SOUNDS FAKE BUT OKAY

of related interest

Ace Voices
What it Means to Be Asexual, Aromantic, Demi or Grey-Ace
Eris Young
ISBN 978 1 78775 698 4
eISBN 978 1 78775 699 1

How to Be Ace
A Memoir of Growing Up Asexual
Rebecca Burgess
ISBN 978 1 78775 215 3
eISBN 978 1 78775 216 0

How to Understand Your Sexuality
A Practical Guide for Exploring Who You Are
Meg-John Barker and Alex Iantaffi
Foreword by Erika Moen
ISBN 978 1 78775 618 2
eISBN 978 1 78775 619 9

Sounds Fake But Okay

An Asexual and Aromantic Perspective
on Love, Relationships, Sex, and
Pretty Much Anything Else

Sarah Costello and Kayla Kaszyca

Jessica Kingsley Publishers
London and Philadelphia

First published in Great Britain in 2023 by Jessica Kingsley Publishers
An imprint of Hodder & Stoughton Ltd
An Hachette UK Company

1

A CIP catalogue record for this title is available from
the British Library and the Library of Congress

ISBN 978 1 83997 001 6
eISBN 978 1 83997 002 3

Printed and bound in the United States by Integrated Books International

Jessica Kingsley Publishers' policy is to use papers that are natural,
renewable and recyclable products and made from wood grown in
sustainable forests. The logging and manufacturing processes are expected
to conform to the environmental regulations of the country of origin.

Jessica Kingsley Publishers
Carmelite House
50 Victoria Embankment
London EC4Y 0DZ

www.jkp.com

For each other

"Queer not as being about who you're having sex with—that can be a dimension of it—but queer as being about the self that is at odds with everything around it and has to invent and create and find a place to speak and to thrive and to live."
—bell hooks*

Contents

Dictionary

Allonormativity The belief that all people are and should be both allosexual and alloromantic.

Alloromantic (allo) A person who experiences romantic attraction. Someone who is not on the aromantic spectrum.

Allosexual (allo) A person who experiences sexual attraction. Someone who is not on the asexual spectrum.

Amatonormativity The belief that all people are better off in an exclusive, monogamous, romantic–sexual relationship, and that everyone is seeking such a relationship.

Aromantic (aro) A person who is aromantic experiences little to no romantic attraction.

Asexual (ace) A person who is asexual experiences little to no sexual attraction. It should be noted that sexual attraction is not the same as sexual desire or a person's libido. Rather, it is who you are or are not attracted to.

Aspectrum (aspec) While asexuality and aromanticism are orientations, they are also spectrums and umbrella terms that serve as a catch-all for a number of other more specific identities. Other sexual orientations that involve little to no sexual attraction (ace, demi, grey, etc.) are included in the asexual spectrum (acespec). Other romantic orientations that involve little to no romantic attraction (aro, demi, grey, etc.) are included in the aromantic spectrum (arospec). When grouped together, these two spectrums are referred to as the aspectrum (aspec). A person who falls on the asexual spectrum and/or aromantic spectrum may be referred to as aspec. It should be noted that there are many more identities within the aspec that are not listed in this dictionary. We have opted to include those which appear most often throughout the book.

Demiromantic (demi) A demiromantic person only experiences romantic attraction to someone once they are platonically or emotionally bonded with that person.

Demisexual (demi) A demisexual person only experiences sexual attraction to someone once they are romantically or emotionally bonded with that person.

Greyromantic A greyromantic person only experiences romantic attraction rarely or weakly. A greyromantic person may also relate to aromanticism but feel that it doesn't fit completely—that they are more in a grey area.

Greysexual A greysexual person only experiences sexual attraction rarely or weakly. A greysexual person may also relate to asexuality but feel that it doesn't fit completely—that they are more in a grey area.

Prologue

The aspec story is a love story. They all are, in the end. There is this idea, this theory that many people have, that those who identify anywhere on the aspectrum—aromantic, asexual, and any of the related labels—are lacking something in their lives. Lacking some strong, incontestable love that is innate to the human experience and therefore makes aspec people not just wrong or unnatural, but something less than human.

This idea, in addition to being a mere misconception, is also complete and utter bullshit. The idea that there is only one type of meaningful love is a ridiculous notion in and of itself. The idea that there is only one type of acceptable existence is even more so.

But the experience of every aspec person is different, and the way we all interact with our identities (whether aspec, otherwise queer, or none of the above) is a deeply personal, introspective process. As such, it is impossible for us to delve into the contents of this book without first introducing you to what we completely unbiasedly view as the greatest love story of all time—our own.

Sarah

I met Kayla at the age of 17, when some random algorithm at University of Michigan Housing placed us in the same dorm room at Alice Lloyd Hall. We were two perfect strangers destined to share a tiny living space as we first stepped into the liminal space between childhood and adulthood, and frankly, things got weird very quickly. Good weird, to be clear—by week two, people, assuming we were longtime friends who had opted to room together in college, were asking us how long we'd known each other, only to be told that we'd met mere days prior. I have always found love at first sight to be an absurd concept, but it cannot be denied that our vibes aligned early on, and we got into something of a groove.

At the time, we both found ourselves stressing about the start of college and all that came with it: difficult classes, making friends, living away from home for the first time. Our sexualities were not anywhere near front of mind. We didn't discuss love and sex in the way that many of our contemporaries did, because we had bigger fish to fry. I'd always thought of myself as something of a late bloomer in this respect, so it didn't faze me.

Then, a few months into freshman year, once I started to wonder if even the so-called "late bloomers" would have bloomed by now and started questioning my own sexuality here and there in the back of my mind—well, I surely didn't tell Kayla. Instead, I sat at my desk in our dorm room adding various aspec-related web pages to a note on my phone vaguely titled "a resources," hyper-aware that Kayla might come back from class at any minute, prepared to click away to another tab as soon as I heard her unlocking the door.

Because these things—love things, sexuality things—weren't something we talked about. We mutually complained about our neighbor across the hall who regularly sexiled his poor roommate, sure, but that was the extent of it.

And yet, Kayla was there as I stressed about my first kiss—a stage kiss for a musical we were both in, which meant I had plenty of time to panic before the dreaded Kiss Rehearsal. She didn't bat an eye when, afterwards, I determined it had been highly anticlimactic.

Months later, Kayla would be the first one to know that I was aro ace. It's not an honor I bestowed on her intentionally, I suppose, but I'm glad she lays claim to that achievement anyway. With all we've done together, both up to that point and in the interim since then, it's fitting that the title be hers.

Kayla

Sarah and I did not come to terms with our identities at the same time. We didn't even start questioning at the same time. Saying that my sexuality wasn't front of mind during our freshman year is the understatement of the century. Until I found out Sarah was aro ace, I had never once questioned my own sexuality.

From my position, it's hard to not believe in some sort of fate, in some kind of higher power that makes sure you meet the right people at the right time. It is undeniable that if Sarah and I had not been randomly placed in room 4005 of Alice Lloyd Hall, we would not be writing this book, and we would not have created a podcast that has given me opportunities I never even dreamed of. But more importantly, and more relevant to this work itself, if I had never met Sarah I doubt that I would have ever discovered my true identity.

It was not until Sarah "came out" (I use this term lightly, as she did not so much come out as make a post on Tumblr that I happened to see) that I started to wonder if I might not be straight after all; if I could be on the asexual spectrum, too. For a while, I ignored this feeling, the questions that appeared in the back of my mind, the lurking thought that perhaps Sarah and I were even more similar than we had initially thought—though this seemed impossible. I was in a committed relationship; I was already having sex. If I was demisexual, as I was starting to question, surely it wouldn't be relevant anyway.

Sarah's account of me from that first year is very kind. It is true that we were both incredibly focused on school. We stayed up late into the night studying, we rarely partied, we got good grades. Even so, I was still interested in boys and dating. In the same dorm room that Sarah sat and researched asexuality, I made out with one of the guys from across the hall (not at the same time, obviously: I respectfully waited for Sarah to be gone for the weekend). While one musical rehearsal gave Sarah her first, anxious kiss, other rehearsals found me unabashedly flirting with the actor who played my love interest. While in most ways Sarah and I are identical, in many key ways we are the opposite. I knew this to be true, so how could it also be true that I might share an identity with her?

In the end, it was true. There are many ways to be aspec, I would learn, and quite a few of those ways include flirting, making out, and hooking up. And so around January of 2018, a year or two after Sarah "came out," after several heartbreaks, a few failed attempts at dating, and some tearful conversations (all of which we'll delve into later), I officially started calling myself demisexual.

Over time, as we gradually became more comfortable with our own identities, we started openly discussing the questions that Sarah always had lurking in the back of her mind. Is making out really that great? How long *is* sex supposed to last? What the hell is the appeal of dick pics? We found the conversations that resulted to be amusing and hoped others would think the same, and because it was 2017, a point in time in which everyone and their mother was starting a podcast, so did we. We called it *Sounds Fake But Okay*. (Because, let's be real, many of the things allosexuals and alloromantics talk about *do* sound profoundly fake. It's just that somehow, over time, we forgot that the rituals behind dating and sex were constructs made up by human beings and eventually, they became hard and fast rules that society imposed on us all.)

The podcast was something we started for fun. We didn't have any grand plans for it and were frankly shocked when we got the rare social media follow from someone we didn't personally know. It did not grow quickly by any stretch of the imagination, but we continued to do it because it was a fun thing to do together.

And yet, with time, we started to gain a small but mighty audience. We began to receive the occasional email from a listener telling us that the podcast had helped them come to terms with their asexuality and/or aromanticism, that it had helped them not feel so alone. The emails, the tweets, and the DMs kept rolling in, and we realized that what we were doing might somehow matter. It seemed that however unintentionally, *Sounds Fake But Okay* had filled what had turned out to be a cavernous podcasting gap in the aspec community. We had found and embedded ourselves in a niche that we hadn't even realized was lacking.

We started taking our role as aspec podcasters more seriously. It wasn't just about us anymore: it was about the broader community who saw themselves in our podcast, who learned from us, who gained comfort from hearing our often-chaotic babbling in their ears.

And because the aspec community is smaller, younger, and more siloed than those of other queer identities (with an organized, identifiable community only really coming to fruition in the early 2000s with the advent of the Asexuality Visibility and Education Network [AVEN]), our little podcast somehow became one of the bigger names in said community. We became activists of sorts, purely on accident. Somewhere along the way, we became experts.

And now, we've found ourselves here.

We should, of course, give the disclaimer that we don't have degrees in queer theory, we weren't trained by some benevolent god of asexuality, and this isn't even our day job (yet). But diving into the discourse of the asexual umbrella and the aspec community at least once a week for years on end and observing your surroundings from an intentionally aspec perspective teaches you a thing or two about the world, how you fit in it, and how it might be changed for the better.

As we've already mentioned, the experience of every aspec

person is different. We are just two people with two very specific experiences (two experiences, we should note, that are inherently cisgender, white, and Western). Nevertheless, we will do our best here to speak to the experiences of many. While the majority of this work will come from our own knowledge, we did feel the need to bring in the voices of others who have more authority on subjects such as polyamory (Chapter 4) and gender identity (Chapter 7).

We wanted to ensure that we had as much diversity among these voices as possible, so instead of just asking the people we knew, we developed a survey through which our listeners and the broader aspec community could share their personal experiences. You'll find their quotes throughout the book, and we hope you learn as much from their perspectives as we have.

Though this is a book about asexuality, it will not be an ace 101 textbook or a historical outline, nor will it focus exclusively on sexual identity in the traditional sense. We of course have chapters focusing on romantic relationships and sex (Chapters 4 and 5 respectively), but we want to discuss topics beyond just sexual activity or who you choose (or don't choose) to date. We will be applying the aspec worldview to topics such as friendship (Chapter 3), family (Chapter 6), housing, and more (Chapter 8).

Throughout this book, we will lend you our own pair of aspec lenses—purple-colored glasses, if you will, inspired by the colors of the asexual flag—with the hope that after seeing what could be, you will be compelled to embrace the aspec perspective in your own life. It's a big undertaking, surely, but don't let that daunt you. Every stumble, fumble, and baby step matters.

Scan this QR code or click on the link below to access a bonus podcast episode about the making of this chapter.

https://www.soundsfakepod.com/sounds-book-but-okay-prologue

CHAPTER 1

Society

In his acceptance speech for Best Score at the 2016 Tony Awards, Lin Manuel-Miranda co-opted a popular phrase to say what would become a well-circulated quote following the ceremony and beyond: "And love is love is love is love is love is love is love is love, cannot be killed or swept aside."

This was a powerful statement in the light of the previous night's Pulse nightclub shooting, when a gunman opened fire on a gay nightclub in Orlando in what would become one of the deadliest mass shootings in modern US history. It was a bold statement made from a tall soapbox that reminded us all that queer love is beautiful, that queer love is worthy, that queer love is precious.

At the time, of course, we agreed. At the time, Sarah, if not Kayla, was already identifying as queer. But it wasn't until over four years and 118 podcast episodes later that Sarah realized that this phrase—"love is love"—also applied to her. That it applies to all aspec people. That it has always applied to loves of all sorts and stripes, romantic and otherwise, and will continue to do so until the end of time.

Earlier we called our story—the story of Sarah and Kayla, Kayla and Sarah—a love story. We say that because it is. It is a story based in love, about two people who love each other, and that's all a love story needs. Our love being purely platonic doesn't make it any less worthy than the romantic–sexual stories we typically think about when discussing love stories (something we'll discuss further in upcoming chapters).

Likewise, the aspec story is a love story because all aspec people, of every identity under the umbrella, experience love. Whether that's a deep connection with a life partner, a moment of pure and unadulterated excitement when seeing a cute dog on the street, or somewhere in between, it's all love.

And yet, this is not a widely accepted notion. Love stories, according to Western society more broadly, are always about romance and sex. An emotional "I love you" between two non-kin characters in a dramatic film is assumed to be an expression of romantic love. Even just using the word *love* in reference to people in the English language implies romantic love unless specified otherwise.

But how the hell did we end up here? And how can we take our socially conditioned, romance- and sex-centric blinders off, start seeing the world through an aspec lens, and begin to build for ourselves a world that is both loving and free of expectation?

Well, step one is realizing how powerful those blinders are to begin with.

Before we dive too deep into the nitty-gritty, we first want to make very clear that when we talk about "society," not just in this chapter but throughout the whole book, we are writing from a Western, English-speaking perspective. We have done our best to cast as wide a net as possible when defining society and discussing what it expects of its participants (willing or unwilling), but the fact remains that we are both white Americans who grew up in the suburbs. It would be irresponsible to pretend that doesn't impact our perception of the social order and what our perceived role is in changing it.

Every person will find themselves face to face with a slightly different social order and set of cultural expectations. Whether or not the society you know looks exactly the same as that which we describe here is less important than being able to dissect and critically read the motivations behind said society. We hope that the key takeaway from this chapter is not "these are the specific structures we must destroy and there is no variation among them," but "here are examples of social structures that are common, broad, and harmful. Here's how we might use our aspec lens to identify and dismantle both them and other structures like them."

Okay, cool? Cool. Let's go.

From the moment any child is conceived, the crushing weight of society has already begun to bear down upon them.

Admittedly, this sounds a bit dramatic. Because ... well, it is. But it's also not necessarily false.

Children are placed into gendered boxes even before they're born—pregnant folks get told by strangers that by the way they're carrying the baby, it *must* be this gender or that. Parents prepare pink nurseries for a girl, blue for a boy. At baby showers, those pregnant with girls receive bows and frilly skirts for the baby, whereas those pregnant with boys receive onesies decorated with cars and trucks and trains.

Once the baby is born, those societal expectations and pressures expand very quickly (along the lines of gender, of course) into the realm of heteronormativity. A young boy befriends a girl in his kindergarten class? Watch out, he's going to be a heartbreaker. Fully grown adults ask children, unprompted, which classmate of theirs they have a crush on. Girls are sexualized before they even hit puberty.

Yes, different cultures impress slightly different expectations and pressures, but the general outline tends to be the same: romance and sex are normal. If you don't feel attraction in the same way that everyone else seems to, not only are you missing out, but there's something wrong with you.

Even progressive communities, those who reject all things heteronormative, tend to be highly allonormative—that is, the fact that someone experiences both sexual attraction and romantic attraction is assumed or at the very least taken for granted. Sure, you're told, you may be queer, but you still experience romantic love and attraction like a *normal* person. At least you're not a robot, a loveless freak.

In a similar vein, many of these supposedly progressive communities also embrace amatonormativity, a term coined by Professor Elizabeth Brake to describe "the widespread assumption that everyone is better off in an exclusive, romantic, long-term coupled relationship, and that everyone is seeking such a relationship."[1] Even those who are sex-positive and embrace and support polyamory often fail to embrace the other end of the spectrum: the idea that romance and sex in general are not a requirement for a fulfilling life.

Before we move any further in this argument, it's important that we first establish that this entire book will be grounded in the premise of the split attraction model (SAM). What the split model describes is an ethos wherein romantic attraction and sexual attraction are *not* the same thing.[a]

It is true that for many people, romantic and sexual attraction are related, and for some it might even be impossible to differentiate between the two. In fact, for the vast majority in society, they are understood to be the same thing (i.e., saying someone is "heterosexual" implies that they are both hetero*romantic* and hetero*sexual*). The fact of the matter, however, is that though the exact location of the line between romantic attraction and sexual attraction may differ from person to person, this line does exist. Further, embracing the split model allows us to dive deeper into understanding the attraction that we may or may not experience. This is why, in aspec communities, people will often list both their romantic and sexual orientation—whether, like Sarah, they carry the same prefix (aromantic and asexual) or whether, like Kayla, they're not the same at all (biromantic and demisexual).

However, the tenets of the split model do not apply only to aspecs, but rather all people. Some people find that they identify as homoromantic bisexual, or panromantic heterosexual—any combination of the identities is possible.

And although they are separate, expectations related to both romance and sex are equally prevalent parts of our social order. They are not weighted equally at every moment, nor do they weigh the same on all genders, but it is important that we recognize that each carries a burden and places pressure on us.

---

a   While we won't delve deeply into attractions outside of romantic and sexual, it should be noted that the SAM also accounts for other types of attraction such as sensual and aesthetic attraction.

Every person, regardless of how woke, educated, or queer, is impacted by these pressures, whether we know it or not.

Sarah

I assumed, for the first decade and a half of my life, that I would someday get married. It was what everyone did, right? It's not like my parents specifically pushed this onto me or ever discussed it with me, but all the examples I saw in the media of successful adults involved a committed and monogamous romantic–sexual partner. No exceptions. Full stop.

Yet in my own life, I knew several fully grown adults who were unmarried and who remained perfectly successful and happy in their own right. One might think I would look to these people as examples, view their lifestyles as alternative options, but instead, young me saw them as outliers. I didn't look down on them, but I didn't aspire to be them either. I would, of course, not follow their grisly path, but embark on the well-trodden byway of my many, many foremothers: marry a nice man, have two and a half kids, buy a house with a white picket fence, live happily ever after. I even imagined what my wedding dress would look like (painfully early 2000s in design) and what I might name my kids (the extensive list detailed both first and middle names).

I continued to think this way well into my teenage years.

Then, in 11th grade and at the ripe old age of 16, I took Advanced Placement English Language and Composition. The teacher was Ms. Burke, a woman who was widely beloved by her students—the *cool* English teacher who, despite being "old" in the eyes of her students (dear reader, she wasn't even middle-aged), was teenager-approved.

Ms. Burke was single, childless, and as far as I could discern, happy with this turn of events; her unfettered lifestyle meant that despite being a woefully underpaid teacher, she was able to spend her summers traveling all around the world. She decorated her classroom walls with pictures of her many travels, and willingly shared stories with us—the places she went, the things she saw, the many strangers who were shocked by her uncovered hair on the streets of Cairo.

Because of all of this, when I looked at her, 16-year-old me saw something new. Ms. Burke was a "real" adult. She was established. She was successful. Yet this was the life she willingly chose—because she looked the burdens of societal expectation and social pressure in the eye and told them *no*. Being single and childless didn't make her some spinster or hag, it made her cool. It meant that she got to do things that my other teachers, with their marriages and children, could not.

And for the first time, it became apparent that that life—the Ms. Burke life—was an option for me. She was tangible proof that you could buck society's expectations and still thrive, that you could be partnerless and childless and still live a fulfilling, exciting life.

Why it was my AP Lang teacher who opened my eyes to this and not members of my own family, I can't say. Perhaps it was the stories of her travels that got me. Perhaps I just needed to learn it from an outsider. Whatever the case, Ms. Burke's mere existence opened a door for me. I wouldn't step through that door for some time, but that didn't matter. Just knowing that it was there, that I could reach out and turn the handle and step through at any moment, transformed my world.

It wasn't until I was much older, when I had come to terms with my identity and finally stepped through that door, that I realized that for all the imagining young me did of my potential stereotypical future, my husband and two and a half kids and white picket fence, I didn't imagine actually living that future.

I didn't imagine what my husband might be like, instead investing my imagination into creating the perfect wedding dress and allowing my future life partner to remain nameless and faceless. I imagined what I might name my children because I have always loved names and naming things, not because I had any interest in actually being a mother.

I didn't truly want any of the things I imagined for my future; I just thought I was supposed to. I imagined the future that was expected of me for no other reason than it was the expectation. But looking to my 11th grade English teacher and realizing I could break away from that, that I could choose the future I wanted, let it take the shape that was right for me without heeding the watchful eyes of Big Brother and society's oppressive expectations—that set me free.

Society is built for couples, in the context of everything from tax benefits and life insurance policies to Spotify discounts and buy-one-get-one couples massages.

We've built our society around the romantic–sexual partnership not only because it's the preferred, idolized way of being in our social order, but also because it's simply the default.

For centuries, it has been expected of essentially all people that once they reach a certain age, they will pair into hetero, monogamous marriages and produce offspring. In many situations, it's more than just an expectation, it's a given. To pursue an alternative lifestyle by choice is outright taboo.

But why?

Coupling for the purpose of reproduction is surely driven in large part by evolutionary instinct. What of the rest of it, though? We'll leave it to the actual scientists to dissect why humans are social pack animals, and we'll leave it to the reply guys of the internet to argue about whether there's any biological merit behind modern gender norms, but there's so much to explore beyond these basic concepts.

Why are romantic relationships inherently valued as greater than platonic relationships? Why is it assumed that just because a person lacks a romantic partner, they must also be lonely? Why is it believed that couples who have children are more productive in society than those without?

Whether or not we have the answers to these questions, of course, is not actually the point. Aspec activists much more academically minded than ourselves have rightfully pointed to capitalism and white supremacy as the source of many of our societal maladies. But on a micro level, identifying straightforward, unambiguous answers to such complex queries is far easier in theory than in practice. What matters is that we're asking the questions, and that we are becoming aware of the way our social order shapes our relationships, our priorities, and our view of the world.

Picture, for example, an old woman. She lives alone, she's never been married, and she's childless. Perhaps she has a few cats. Now, don't think. Just let your gut guide you. What are you picturing?

A lonely spinster? A grumpy old hag? A Disney villainess, even?

If what you pictured was anything but a negative depiction of this woman, then we applaud you, because you're a step ahead of the rest of us. Society conditions us to believe that this woman must be lonely, or mean, or otherwise unsavory, simply because she is existing outside the norm.

But if that old spinster with her cats is content, fulfilled, and not hurting anyone, who are we to tell her she's doing it wrong? Who are we to tell her that she's "missing out" on something? Why must her happiness look the same as everyone else's?

Alternative lifestyles need not be what you're stuck with if you can't achieve the marriage, kids, and white picket fence—they can instead be what you choose. If living alone with a handful of cats sounds good to you, then by all means, do it. If it doesn't, don't. If it does, but then you change your mind and decide you want to pursue a different path instead, that's fine, too.

In the end, a heteronormative society benefits from staying heteronormative. It's easier for those who fit the heteronormative bill when those couple-centric pillars of society remain entrenched, because it means the world of tax benefits and Spotify discounts continues to be built for people like them. That's why these norms endure, not because they have any inalienable basis in fact or truth.

Okay, sure, you may be thinking, this is all very good and nice, but some of you may also note that there is still an elephant in the room. Thus far we've mentioned a few times a so-called "aspec lens"—and will continue to do so throughout this book, as it is the essence of and engine behind our entire text—but what the hell does that actually mean? What is the aspec lens and how do we use it? Even for folks who may already be familiar with the concept, it doesn't have a clear, official definition within aspec communities. It's not a particularly easy thing to define— after all, even in a book explicitly about the aspec lens, it was necessary for us to provide a full chapter of context before even breaching the subject of its meaning. But now that you have that necessary background, we'll finally define for you what we mean by the aspec lens in the context of this book.

To view something through the aspec lens is to strip it of all societal expectations. To approach the world eyes wide open about how profound the social pressure is on every aspect of life and every minor decision we make. To know that what we are taught is right is not the only way to be, that just because your experience of the world is less common doesn't make it automatically unnatural or wrong.

It is to reject the premise that we should act a certain way just because "that's the way it's always been." To look at the world as objectively as we can muster, and to let that guide our decisions and opinions.

When people first learn about asexuality and the broader umbrella of aspec identities, it can often be difficult for them to wrap their heads around. It's far less straightforward than understanding, for example, what it means to be gay. A straight person can look to a gay person and say okay, they're just like me, except they feel attraction to the same gender. A straight woman can understand and empathize with the attraction that gay men feel towards other men, because she feels that exact same type of attraction to men, too. But for people, whether straight or not, to learn that some people don't feel any such attraction at all and can still be perfectly fulfilled—that can flip their world on its head. And with any luck, their reaction to learning this won't be pushback, but a lightbulb moment. A moment of understanding that *Oh, there is a whole other abundance of perfectly valid ways of existing that I had not previously considered.*

Quick, before it's gone—capture that lightbulb moment. Condense it down to its most basic essence. Mold it into a lens through which to view the whole world. Dye it purple, if you so please.

This is your aspec lens.

A therapist once told Sarah that we humans are not benefitted by the pressure of feeling like we should do one thing or another. Merely telling ourselves that we *should* quit procrastinating our work, or that we *should* do the laundry, or that we *should* eat a vegetable instead of another plate of toaster waffles, doesn't make us *want* to do those things. It just makes us feel guilty that we're not doing those things. Maybe some people are spurred to action by that guilt (though we certainly aren't), but no matter the outcome, the weight of that guilt isn't healthy.

As Sarah began to embrace that which she and her therapist had discussed, she acquired something of a mantra for herself: *don't should.* And the truth of the matter is that this mantra can apply to all aspects of life, well beyond the bounds of work, laundry, and vegetable consumption.

Feeling like you should get married, for example, just because everyone expects you to? Nope, *don't should.* Because what does *should*-ing do for us, anyway, aside from dropping the heavy weight of expectation onto our shoulders and boxing us into a pre-prescribed future? What benefit do we garner from being shamed for not having had our first kiss by 16 (or 18, or ever)?

To be clear, we do not mean to imply that anyone who genuinely wants and strives for the things that fulfill societal expectations is any lesser than anyone else. If someone really wants a monogamous marriage, two and a half kids, and a house with a white picket fence, more power to them. We would never look down on it if that's what brings someone love and fulfillment. But they ought to be seeking out those things because they actually *want* them, not because that's what society tells them they should want. It's all about making conscious choices rather than passive ones.

Still, for those who do wish to fly in the face of society, we recognize that it is far easier said than done, and even attempting to do so is not necessarily a realistic path for all people. Any number of variables can factor into the barriers people may face: race, cultural background, religion, class, gender, disability, and so forth. Just as we don't intend to judge or look down upon anyone who seeks the white picket fence life of their own free will, we also don't intend to judge or look down upon anyone who wants to buck the status quo but can't for reasons outside of their control. If you fall into this category, know that even if you are unable to change your behavior, just wearing your purple-colored glasses is a huge achievement. Viewing the world from the aspec perspective does make a positive impact on how you act and treat those around you. This holds true even if you aren't in a place to burn the whole system down, now or ever—and we hope all of our readers remember that.

Just as *don't should* remains the mantra of our lives, it will also be the throughline of this book. Everything we say, when broken down to the smallest possible pieces, comes back to *don't should*. Everything about the aspec lens, really, comes back to *don't should*.

On the surface, this sounds basic. Tired. Clichéd, even. The entry-level feminist adages that we've all heard before—"down with the patriarchy," "my body, my choice," "don't trap yourself in a loveless marriage"—these are all different incarnations of *don't should*. And don't get us wrong, they're absolutely right. But the aspec lens asks us to dig even deeper than just pieces of sisterly advice or the sorts of things we write on signs at a feminist protest.

It's easy to say you reject social constructs, but it's another beast entirely to live that in your everyday life. Being aspec is not just about an identity or a group, but about experiencing the world in a different way from everyone else. For an aro ace like Sarah, she's not choosing to stay single as a political act or to be a #GirlBoss, but because the attraction is simply not there, and as a result dating is of no interest to her. To give in and follow the heteronormative expectation would be to live a lie.

That's what makes the aspec lens so special—it's taking that punk attitude, that rejection of social norms and expectations, and fully immersing yourself in it. It's about applying this mindset to every aspect of your life, not just when it's easy or convenient. And the fact of the matter is that it's frequently neither of those things.

Some may be inclined to romanticize the experience of rejecting society, focusing on the positive feelings of freedom, but in reality the process of freeing oneself of societal expectation, fully embracing the mantra of *don't should*, and wearing your aspec glasses 24/7 can be incredibly painful. Punk rockers may enter their lifestyle by choice—but with the realization of their identity, aspecs are thrust into this brave new world without much say in the matter. They are certainly not required to act on everything they learn, but after first encountering the aspec lens and realizing it's a part of who they are, it's difficult for any aspec to leave it behind entirely.

Now, if any of our readers have acquired some sort of complex in the past few paragraphs, thinking that you're superior because you've loosened the chains of societal expectation in a way that your peers haven't, or thinking that as an aspec this makes you better than allos, we kindly ask you to pipe down. Learning to embrace the aspec lens in both the big and small of everyday life is a process. As we established earlier, societal expectation and social pressure to adhere to the norm is pressing down on us from all sides at all times. Everyone has their own unique hurdles and roadblocks, and if there's a person out there who's already successfully summited this particular mountain, it's certainly neither of us.

In the meantime, all we can do is keep the aspec lens front of mind and do our best to acknowledge and resist the powerful expectations and pressures that are pervasive in every nook and cranny of society. So, with that in mind, we'll remind you one more time: *don't should.*

Seriously, don't.

Scan this QR code or click on the link below to access a bonus podcast episode about the making of this chapter.

https://www.soundsfakepod.com/sounds-book-but-okay-society

CHAPTER 2

Yourself

In the queer community, there are two stories that are nearly universal. The first is the infamous coming out story: sometimes triumphant, other times gut-wrenching. The other and more often joyful story is the story of someone's queer awakening. The tale of what made that person realize they were queer.

For some, that realization may have been a high school friendship that, come to think of it, was a bit more codependent and physical than a typical friendship. For others, maybe it was an oddly passionate affinity for the rivalry between Kim Possible and Shego. And for others yet, perhaps it was a moment when they looked across the bar, saw a cute guy, and had that classic romance novel *oh* moment. No matter the details, there is one thing that these stories have in common—the presence of another person, be that a real human or a fictional character.

So what does that story look like when you're on the asexual and/or aromantic spectrums? When, by definition, that *oh* moment never comes, or only comes once in a lifetime under a very specific set of circumstances? Unlike many other queer folks, an asexual or aromantic awakening is not noticing that you are attracted to someone that you didn't expect to be attracted to, but slowly realizing that that attraction has yet to come.

It's realizing, as Sarah did, that if you were a late bloomer, certainly you would have bloomed by now.

To realize you are aspec is to one day think to yourself, "You know, I've never actually had a celebrity crush" or, "Hm, I think there's only one person in my entire life who I've ever been sexually attracted to." And then to think, "Well, now what do I do?" Because unlike a man realizing he is gay, for example, you can't necessarily waltz into a gay bar to experiment and see how your newfound attraction feels.

Of course, there is nothing stopping an aspec person from participating in this type of physical experimentation. In a way, an aspec person's entire life before they realize they're aspec is experimenting. For many, it is years of attempting to find that attraction or wondering what's wrong with them, why their relationships don't feel the way everyone else's seem to feel.

So instead of going to that gay bar, aspecs are often left to bravely waltz into the recesses of their minds to think deeply about the feelings that they have or have not felt for their entire lives. Hopefully, in doing so they'll pick up those purple-colored glasses and try them on for size.

Kayla

If recent sessions of therapy have taught me anything, it's that I spend a fair amount of time suppressing my emotions. Not the type of suppression you might be thinking of, the type you'd attribute to a stereotypical strong and silent father who you've only seen cry at a funeral. No, my suppression is more internal. It's less about keeping myself from expressing emotions outwardly (that would be impossible, I cry far too easily). Instead, it's the type that causes me to ensure every hour of my day is filled, the type that causes me to fear silence because if there's nothing to distract me then maybe, just maybe, I'll have to listen to the voices inside my head. This is fine in small doses, I suppose. Everyone needs a distraction from life now and again. But as they say, all things are best in moderation. Because it turns out that if you don't stop distracting, if you don't take time to talk to yourself, sit with yourself, and let yourself think, you might miss out on some pretty big revelations.

I hope you can see where I'm going with this. Though I've only recently realized just how many emotions and issues I've suppressed, my chronic suppression has impacted every part of my life. When it came to figuring out my sexuality, it was my biggest obstacle. Even though I had everything going for me (a podcast about asexuality, a best friend who was already out, a supportive group of queer friends), my coming-out process was still drawn out, and that's because I refused to think about it.

As I shared in our Prologue, I first started considering demisexuality when I was in a relationship with a boy who I had been dating for a long time and was already sexually attracted to. This gave me a relatively legitimate reason to put my sexuality out of mind for the moment, if not forever. In my naive, 19-year-old brain, I thought we would be together forever, that I would never need to form attraction to another person.

Friends, would you be surprised if I told you this was not the case? That we did in fact break up? Of course you wouldn't be, you're much smarter than I was at the time. Nevertheless, we did break up and I was left with no excuses, no reason to not finally figure out if I was demisexual. And yet I'm sure you will also not be surprised to learn that I opted not to do that.

If you're a diligent listener of *Sounds Fake But Okay*, this may confuse you slightly. You might say, "But Kayla, you talked about how you might be demisexual in the very first episode. You were questioning from the very beginning." And yes, you'd be right. In the first episode of the podcast, before I had even broken up with that boyfriend, I said, "I feel like sometimes I might be demisexual, which means I have to be romantically and emotionally attached to someone before I'm sexually attracted to them." I made statements like this in countless episodes, both before and after the break up.

But that was Podcast Kayla, the Kayla who sat down with her aro ace friend for an hour each week to talk about sexuality in depth and personally. Podcast Kayla thought about her demisexuality, considered it as an option, and saw the benefits of immersing herself in the community. Real Life Kayla, though? The one who had to go to class, who was dating in the college scene, who had friends and family completely removed from the community? She thought about demisexuality as little as possible. When the microphones were turned off and she left Sarah's room after recording, she neatly packed Podcast Kayla and her sexuality back into a box and shoved it to the back of her brain where she wanted it to belong.

I guess you could consider this dishonest, lying even, but I have to admit I feel no guilt in that regard. I think we all have enough media literacy to know that no one shares their full truth on the internet, especially influencers and content creators, which I suppose I should lump myself in with.

But now that we're here, now that I'm pulling the curtain back slightly and sharing a bit more of Real Life Kayla's reality, I might as well share what was really going through my mind at that time and what finally forced me to accept my demisexuality.

During the post-break up era, during the time where I was questioning my demisexuality but intentionally not taking the label, in some episode of the podcast I said something to the effect of, "Once I start dating again I'll probably have to confront the fact that I might be demisexual." This may be one of the biggest lies I told. Because while Podcast Kayla was resolute to understand her identity before jumping back into the dating scene, Real Life Kayla already *was* dating again, or at least "talking to someone" (whatever that means in terms of modern dating), and as we all now know, I was *not* confronting my demisexuality.

This was, of course, not the healthiest option. This may be obvious to most, but trying to date while actively suppressing a part of your sexuality can be incredibly painful. I suffer from relatively severe anxiety in day-to-day life, and the new "situationship" that I found myself in with my deskmate from MEMS 375 did not do my mental state any favors.

That isn't to say that the relationship wasn't fun. It had all the staples of a good college fling—daily texts, flirting, study sessions, making my roommates uncomfortable by making out in the living room, watching *Mindhunter*, etc. But I'm sure you've noticed the missing piece in this perfect college fling: the actual hooking up. Trust me, I noticed it too, and that was the true cause of my anxiety about the situation. On multiple occasions, this fear of the "missing element" sent me into full-on panic attacks. Unfortunately, my panic attacks often involve vomiting, which made the panicked situations I found myself in even worse.

If you'll allow me, I'd like to take a brief pause here to apologize to Nikola, that dear deskmate from MEMS 375. Nikola, when I arrived at your house that one night when you invited me over to study, I did not run to the bathroom to pee after a long walk across campus. No. Instead, I ran to your bathroom to vomit and panic and wonder if you had actually invited me over to have sex rather than study Nordic mythology. On the one hand, I hope to God this is the first you're learning of this. On the other, I realize how strange it must be to discover this in this fashion. Either way, we carry on.

My panic about sex was, of course, directly related to my demisexuality. Nikola and I had only just started "seeing each other." I was not sexually attracted to him yet and I didn't know if I ever would be. At the same time, I was painfully aware of the college hook up scene I found myself in. It wasn't exactly the norm to wait six months to have sex for the first time like I had with my previous boyfriend.

At every moment I was worried that Nikola would try to initiate something I wasn't ready for. Obviously, the option to say no was always there, but that would be awkward. And not only that, but it would also force me to confront the question of "why." Why was the answer no? Why wasn't I interested? Why wasn't I sexually attracted to him? These were questions that I was not ready to answer. These were questions that Podcast Kayla might be prepared for, but Real Life Kayla certainly was not. To Nikola's credit, he didn't ever try anything. It's entirely possible that I was just flattering myself by thinking he would. It's even more possible that he saw the ever-present look of fear in my eyes and knew it wasn't a good idea.

No matter the reasoning and despite there being no clear signs that sex was imminent, my stress persisted. Deep in the back of my mind, I knew that I was demisexual and I knew that the casual dating scene wasn't for me, but I kept shoving those feelings down. I kept convincing myself that casual dating is what I wanted, that I didn't need to jump immediately into a committed relationship, that I could just hook up with someone without having larger emotions or attractions attached.

I continued on in this manner for quite some time. I pushed through the anxiety attacks, impatiently waiting for the racing heart, the sweaty brow, and the uneasy stomach to subside so that I could continue on my merry way. Ultimately, I think it was the exhaustion that finally broke me down and made me realize that at some point this had to stop. Exhaustion, and the college student godsend that is winter break.

Winter break that year not only brought me many miles away from Nikola but also many miles away from the kind of pressure that only a college campus can provide. I was now safely in my small hometown, where there is nothing to do but sit on your parents' couch, think, and perhaps take a walk around your favorite grocery store. Separated from the emotions of the situation, basking in the mental freedom that comes after a brutal set of finals, and bored out of her mind, Real Life Kayla finally pulled her sexuality out of that box and got to work.

This work wasn't fast, nor was it easy. I vividly remember crying in the backseat of my parents' car during that break as I texted Sarah that I didn't want to be demisexual. I insisted that life would be so much easier if I wasn't. If I wasn't demisexual, I could just continue on like a "normal" person, I could even date the way other college kids dated. Sarah, of course, wasn't having any of that. She set me straight (or set me demi, you could say).

When break was finally over and we went back to school, there was a part of me that wanted to shove that demisexuality back down, to continue my unconvincing performance as an allosexual person. But I knew I couldn't do that. So, when I got back to campus, I stopped seeing Nikola. It wasn't anything formal or dramatic, at least not to my memory—more of a mutual ghosting situation. I knew then that it just wouldn't work.

He was looking to date casually, I needed to commit, and both of those needs were and are completely valid. To continue whatever sort of relationship we had was not what either of us needed or wanted. There was nothing wrong with either of us, there was nothing wrong with either of these needs. Different people need different things from relationships.

I was sad, of course. I was heartbroken to not only lose a situationship and person I genuinely enjoyed, but also to say goodbye to a "normal" life or "normal" college experience. That life was never a good fit for me, of course, but the realization that you are so intrinsically different from your peers is never an easy pill to swallow. In the end, though, it was worth it because after that winter break, I finally started calling myself demisexual. After that winter break, Podcast Kayla and Real Life Kayla took their first steps towards merging into one complete person.

We hope it goes without saying that the story told above is not universal. The way this story ends, with Kayla finally accepting that she is demisexual, is not the end of every queer or aspec person's queer awakening story, nor should it be. It's important for us to note here that there is absolutely nothing wrong with not labeling your sexuality. If you aren't comfortable with a label, do not take one on. However, when you choose to not label yourself, make sure you're doing it because that's what you really want, not because you, like Kayla, are too afraid to learn something new about yourself.

At a glance, Kayla's story may seem to fall in line with the phrase uttered at the end of every episode of *RuPaul's Drag*

Race—"If you can't love yourself, how in the hell are you gonna love somebody else? Can I get an amen?" That is not our intention and unfortunately, we will not be giving RuPaul an "amen" on this one. As hundreds of think pieces have said before, this sentiment is not always a healthy one, nor is it even necessarily true. It puts forth the idea that people who don't have self-confidence, who may be mentally ill, or who are struggling to accept themselves are unable to love and care for others. As two mentally ill people who love many people very deeply, we know this to be untrue.

In Kayla's case, it was not a lack of self-love that got in the way of a budding relationship, it was a lack of self-understanding and self-knowledge. Without a clear understanding of her wants and boundaries, without even an ounce of knowledge of what her ideal relationship would look like or how her attraction formed and worked, she floundered. She was unable to communicate to a potential partner, and more importantly to herself, what she truly needed. This understanding, this self-awareness, this stronger relationship with herself that she once sorely lacked, only came with time and with the acceptance of her sexuality.

Having this kind of strong relationship with yourself is not a mandatory prerequisite for being aspec. It does feel, however, that it is almost a side effect. As we have said, asexuality and its broader umbrella of related identities is a complete brain bender. It takes everything we thought we knew about the world and turns it on its head. To not just understand this, but also realize that such a subversive identity applies to you, can be painful. It can be enough to cause you to wish you were "normal" or "like everybody else."

For many aspecs, whether they view their orientation as a large part of their identity or not, coming to terms with their identity often involves an uncomfortable amount of soul searching and self-questioning, the kind that Kayla went through. For your entire life, you may have believed that you need to have sex and/ or romance, to have romantic–sexual relationships, to feel that weird tingly sensation that somehow maps onto attraction. Now that you realize this isn't true, that maybe you don't even like those things, where do you go? And who are you?

Though this line of thinking can, and does, apply to the questioning of any orientation, it can feel incredibly intense for aspec people. This may seem dramatic, but just remember that when you realize you're asexual, you realize that the world has lied to you. This realization can lead to a rabbit hole of questions: "If I'm not sexually attracted to people, or if I at least don't experience sexual attraction often, what does my romantic attraction look like? Now that I've learned that society's rules mean nothing, should I start to investigate my gender?" We'll get into those questions a bit more later.

Unfortunately, there is no magic cure for the stress that questioning your sexuality (or your romantic orientation) induces. There is no multistep program that you can walk through that will spit you out on the other side with a new identity. No, this is a path you have to pave on your own. Of course, there may be others to help you—maybe a queer friend who has already come out, a trusted family member, the internet, or maybe even us. But no journey is the same. Perhaps your friend has known they were queer since they were five, or a lightbulb switched one day in high school and they just knew, or maybe it took them two years of introspection and thinking to finally land on an identity, just to realize they were wrong and start using a new label a month later.

All of these experiences are completely valid, but the important thing to remember is that you can't compare your experience with anyone else's. This can be difficult, of course, especially if your questioning is drawn out or particularly painful. It is easy to become frustrated with yourself, to wonder if there's something wrong with you, to be envious of those who just seem to figure themselves out in a snap.

So, if you do find yourself in this position, here is the small bit of advice we can give you: first, do not assume that someone figured their identity out quickly. It may seem that way from the outside, but it is very possible that they were shielding what they really went through, just as Kayla did. Remember this if you ever start to feel jealous. Second, identity can be fluid. It's okay if your identity changes—it doesn't make however you previously identified any less valid. Your labels may never change, or they may change many times throughout your life, and both experiences are completely normal.

Finally, it is okay to be confused, to not love your identity or yourself right away, or to wish you were different sometimes. These feelings are natural, and in moderation, they are healthy. In the media, we see depictions of queer people who are happy and prideful, who are willing to shout their identities from the rooftops and wear a pride flag on their shirts. This doesn't have to be you. Not now, not ever. Take questioning one day at a time and know that there is no rush. You're not going anywhere, so there's always time to learn more about yourself.

As much as we'd like it to, the questioning process and even the self-knowledge process never truly ends. Just ask Kayla who, in the middle of writing a book about her own identity, started to question her own romantic orientation. We have yet to meet a person who is 100 percent confident with their identity or 100 percent sure of who they are as a person. We are humans, after all, ever evolving and always complicated. But what does this mean for us? That there is never truly an outcome? Never an answer that comes from all this questioning? Not necessarily. There may be an answer for now, a label you land on that you feel most comfortable with, even if some days you aren't quite sure if you're right. And there's the stronger relationship you've built with yourself that you will continue to build. In the end, hopefully getting to know the real you, or at least the real you for now, makes the sometimes painful questioning process at least a bit more worth it.

Sarah—A gastronomical, metaphorical interlude

Imagine yourself as a pie. Whatever type you like—apple, pumpkin, chicken pot, or even just a plain old inedible pie chart for the more mathematically inclined.

Each piece of that pie is a piece of you, a necessary component in creating the full picture of who you are. But not all pieces of your personal pie need be the same size, nor does your pie need to be able to map cleanly onto anyone else's. For some people, their romantic and/or sexual identity is a huge part of their pie, a bigger piece than their career or their hobbies or their love of La Croix. For others, their orientation is just a sliver of their personal pie: ever-present and still a crucial ingredient in building the whole you, but dwarfed by other, much larger pieces.

This is, of course, an imperfect metaphor. It's not like any one person is 30 percent gay and 20 percent mother and 50 percent Detroit Red Wings fan and 0 percent anything else—a person is many things at once, and you can't put a number on any of them. Moreover, as people change and grow, the size of any one piece in their pie can fluctuate.

Having your orientation take up a larger piece of the pie doesn't make you any more queer than someone like me, whose sexual identity is a rather small part of my Sarah Pie. In spite of talking about aspec issues weekly on *Sounds Fake But Okay* and literally writing the book that you're currently reading about the aspec lens, I don't think about my orientation all that often. It's not a part of me that has a huge impact on my life or how I live it. After all, I did decide that the marriage, two and a half kids, white picket fence life wasn't for me long before I ever knew I was aro ace. Who's to say my day-to-day life would be significantly different at all if I identified as panromantic pansexual, or biromantic homosexual, or heteroromantic asexual?

I am infinite amounts aromantic and infinite amounts asexual. So is every other aro ace person, regardless of how big their aro ace piece of pie is. So is every other queer person infinite amounts queer. It's not about *how* aspec (or otherwise queer) we are, but to what extent we choose to make that a part of us. It's about how much real estate we deem pertinent to give it in our personal pie, and there is no right or wrong.

We get a lot of conflicting information from society on what the relationship with the self ought to look like. On one hand, we have RuPaul and her compatriots who will unequivocally tell us that we can't love others until we learn to love ourselves. On the other hand, there are the Holier-Than-Thous who demand we value service and selflessness above all else, even at the expense of one's own self-care and wellbeing.

But as we discussed in the previous chapter, society and

its nice, comfortable status quo does not always have our best interests in mind. And what the aspec lens tells us is that there is always a third option: ignore society, forge your own path, and do what feels best for you.

And although up to this point we have spoken primarily about the aspec experience in regard to the self, all we have said about it is by no means limited to aspecs—as we've noted, aspec identities and this level of self-reflection just tend to come as a package deal.

The time many aspecs are forced to take looking in on themselves and learning to understand their motivations is a time of self-reflection that many allos don't partake in, simply because they don't feel they need to. After all, if the world is built for and around people like you, why bother with questioning your place or identity within it? But no matter your background, whether you're queer, straight, or questioning, there is something to be gained from taking a closer look at the self and gaining a better understanding of what you want and need to thrive.

Returning to Kayla's complicated situationship with her deskmate, we know now how much she would have benefitted from a deeper understanding of herself, her wants, and her needs in that situation. Now many years out from discovering her demisexuality, she has been able to have relationships that, while not perfect, were made better by clear communication and an understanding of what exactly she needed from them.

And this is not an effect that is unique to Kayla. Although the reality of dating while aspec can certainly be difficult, many respondents to our survey also emphasized the advantages.

I think aspec people think a lot about what traits they want their partner to have ... when it comes to sex but also romantic viewpoints, etc. I get the feeling that aspec people think a lot about sexuality in general and are educated in it, to have better insight in their partners. (Franz—he/him—asexual, biromantic)

I'd say dating as an aspec person probably has the benefit that most of us have a pretty complex relationship with sex/romance/ attraction, because most of us had to really question ourselves and do a bunch of research before we even knew asexuality/ aromanticism even existed. So I'd say most of us know ourselves very well in that regard. (Leo—any—demisexual, demiromantic)

We know about ourselves and what we don't and do want in a relationship more than allos know themselves. In our journey to realise our aspec identity, we learn and discuss the ins and outs of consent, kink, and the person-specific essentials of a lifelong partnership. (Amie M Marie—she/her—asexual, biromantic)

And while these quotes pertain specifically to dating and romance, this is merely an example. A deeper understanding of self can vastly improve any relationship, no matter the kind.

Obviously, knowing yourself cannot solve all your problems, nor can it eliminate whatever barriers you may have to truly loving yourself (that's what we talk to therapists for, folks). Nor is it a one-and-done situation—a successful relationship with the self, like any other relationship, is one that must be built up and continuously reinforced.

Like any habit, you will not pick this up in one day. You will not suddenly remember to check in with yourself regularly, to ask yourself questions, to get to know yourself. Unfortunately, you will never be perfectly successful at this either. We certainly aren't. But trust us, just reading this book, this chapter even, is an enormous first step towards a fuller relationship with yourself. So keep going.

Scan this QR code or click on the link below to access a bonus podcast episode about the making of this chapter.

https://www.soundsfakepod.com/sounds-book-but-okay-yourself

CHAPTER 3

Friendship

S ay you have a friend named Tina. You and Tina have known each other for a few years, you have plenty of mutual friends, and you talk often. You're pretty close, all things considered. Then, Tina finds herself in a romantic–sexual[a] relationship. At first, she tells you all about her new partner: the things she likes about them, the details about their first date, how the relationship is going. She starts spending a *lot* of time with this new partner, but you just brush it off as a honeymoon phase.

But then, over time, you just ... stop hearing from her. Tina doesn't reach out to you, and when you reach out to her, she's not as engaged as she used to be. Maybe you make plans, but she flakes on you to see her partner instead, even though they spend every day together and you and Tina haven't seen each other in a month. You ask around with some of your mutual friends, and it turns out she's doing the same thing to them.

A few months pass. Maybe you keep trying to reach out to

---

a For the purposes of this chapter, we will be tying these terms together because this is how they are viewed by society at large. That said, sex is not a necessary component of the equation—a romantic relationship without sex is still viewed as greater than a platonic relationship by the broader social order.

Tina, maybe you don't, but either way, what was once a robust friendship is now something of a ghost town. She continues to spend all of her time with her partner. Then one day, out of the blue, she reaches out again—Tina and her partner have broken up. Without them in her life, she's suddenly interested in being friends with you again. Perhaps you try to mend your relationship and comfort her, but it feels a bit ... odd. Unbalanced. After all, where was she when *you* needed comfort these past few months?

But after a brief time, the story takes another hard left. Tina and her partner are back together—maybe it was just a misunderstanding taken to an extreme and they never split up after all, or maybe they were able to reconcile their differences, but whatever the case, Tina returns to the loving arms of her partner and once again leaves you in the dust.

As it turns out, your friendship only had value to Tina when she was single. Your platonic bond only mattered to her when she wasn't in a romantic–sexual coupling. It was more than just a honeymoon phase or a bit of flakiness—in the end, she simply valued her romantic–sexual partnership more than she valued her platonic ones, full stop.

Unfortunately, this hypothetical friendship you experienced with Tina is a nearly universal story.

Sure, the details are malleable, not every person has experienced every step of it, and it's based on anecdotal evidence rather than a peer-reviewed academic study. (Although if someone wants to do such a study, be our guest. Both metaphorically and literally: we would love to have you on *Sounds Fake But Okay* and hear all about it.)

But the point is, if no part at all of the above story resonates with you, you certainly have a friend, a neighbor, or a coworker with whom it does. Or maybe *you're* the Tina in the situation and you're due for some self-reflection—but that's a topic for another book (and perhaps a therapist).

Our society tells us that there is a clear ranking of importance in the types of relationships any human has, and in this ranking, the romantic-sexual relationship *always* comes before the platonic. In this ranking, other variables do not matter.

Some people, like Tina, will take this to an extreme, dropping their platonic friends as soon as a potential romantic-sexual partner shows any ounce of interest. But even the more evolved folks (or perhaps put a little kinder, the more thoughtful folks) who would never do such a thing are not immune to the thinking that seeps into our minds and insists that romantic-sexual relationships must always reign supreme.

But why? Why, other than that it's merely the state of our heteronormative, allonormative, patriarchal status quo? Decentering the romantic-sexual relationship in our broader conversations about human connection is an absolutely crucial aspect of adopting the aspec lens.

In saying this, we don't mean to disparage or dismiss the value, depth, or importance of "traditional" romantic-sexual relationships. For a great many people, the relationship they have with a romantic-sexual partner is, in fact, the most intimate and important relationship in their life. But society likes to make us think that romantic relationships are inherently better, deeper, and/or more valuable than other relationships just by nature of being romantic, and this could not be further from the truth.

When we say decenter romantic-sexual relationships, we do not mean toss them out the window, never to be seen again. What we mean is that each relationship any one person has should be considered on its own merits—the strongest or most important relationship in your life should take that title because of the bond you share with the other person (or people), not merely because you kiss them or have sex with them.

Each individual relationship has its own unique place in our lives, and we do not benefit from separating the different types of relationships into tiered planes of existence just because society tells us we should.

In fact, even in recent history, society has not always done so. In a 2020 article in *The Atlantic* focused on those who prioritize friendship over romance, Rhaina Cohen discusses "romantic friends," a concept that was fairly widespread from the 18th to early 20th centuries in Europe and America: passionate, same-sex relationships that were not hindered by or even placed on the backburner because of marriage.[2] There is modern speculation around many of these relationships that they were, in fact, simply queer romantic–sexual partnerships shielded by the guise of intimate friendship. And perhaps some were—after all, the idea of homosexuality as we know it today really didn't take shape until the 20th century, after the heyday of romantic friendships. But it's also possible, and even likely, that many of these romantic friendships really were just intimate platonic relationships that existed in a time where people were freer to have strong, lasting platonic partnerships alongside traditional romantic–sexual ones.

However, as society has changed, the sexes have integrated, and the understood difference between gender and sexuality has become more pronounced, it seems we've left the idea of romantic friendship behind. Instead, Western society has embraced a worldview that places platonic friendship distinctly on the second tier, always playing second fiddle to the almighty romance.

Sarah

As an aro ace, I don't fear dying alone. In fact, if we're defining *alone* as "lacking a long-term romantic–sexual partner," I rather expect to. But *alone* and *lonely* are not synonymous. And in the time since I've come to terms with my identity, one fear has plagued me above all others: the fear of platonic abandonment.

Quite luckily, in my case this fear doesn't stem from a neglected childhood, absent parent, or scarring divorce—instead, this fear had been branded into my very being by society herself.

Why? Because "bros before hoes" and "chicks before dicks" only seem to apply prior to marriage or some other long-term commitment. Once the rings are exchanged and "me" turns to "us," it's perfectly acceptable for that union to take precedence in every context, no questions asked. And when you start making decisions as a unit, it's simply easier to make those decisions alongside other units. Married couples hang out with other married couples. Families with kids go on vacation with other families with kids. Going out for drinks with the girls becomes getting a babysitter and going on a double date. And after all, no one likes a third wheel—or in this case, a fifth.

Perhaps this is an oversimplification: not all people, of course, are wont to do this. But the fact of the matter is that whether it is done intentionally or not, it is normal to do this. It is accepted to do this. And no matter how many times Kayla attempts to assuage my fears that this won't happen to me, I cannot leave those fears behind.

Before the mommy bloggers of the world come after me for shaming their families and disparaging their honor, I'd like to note that I understand why, to a certain extent, some of this happens naturally. Sure, a married parent certainly won't have as many shared life experiences with an unmarried, childless friend as they may have had back in their college days. It's hard to plan a mutually enjoyable beach vacation with a friend when your plans are to get sloshed by the ocean, but your friend and their partner need to supervise, entertain, and otherwise maintain the life and safety of a four-year-old whose swimming skills leave something to be desired.

My point is merely that the habitual prioritization of relationships with other coupled friends over single friends is yet another example of our social order asserting the apparently automatic supremacy of romantic–sexual relationships. Of its assertion that if maintaining platonic relationships gets too hard—if your lives don't look enough like each other's or fit together like perfect puzzle pieces—well, maybe those platonic relationships just aren't worth it.

And that's really what takes root at the stem of this fear, which I've found to be rather prevalent among the other aromantics of the world. That once our friends find their "person," their long-term romantic–sexual partner(s), we will be left in the dust. That we will be demoted to a second-tier relationship, where, if it gets too hard to make time or meet up, if life gets in the way, we will be deprioritized further and further until we are abandoned altogether.

For those of us who don't anticipate ever having a life partner of our own, we fear that we will live and die in that second tier. That we will never be anyone's priority. That we will miss out on a certain level of intimacy and love in our lives, not because of our identity, but because the people around us seem unable to grasp that platonic relationships might be worth prioritizing, too.

Now, this interlude is not meant to be Sarah's therapy session. The reason I share all of the above is to give an insight into my personal experience as an aro ace person.

Although intentionally wearing my aspec glasses can help

temporarily deprogram my socially ingrained, heteronormative defaults and reorient me in the world, there are also certain aspects of the aspec lens that I cannot take off even if I try. Maybe for you, dear reader, the concept of such a deep fear of platonic abandonment feels all very detached, an objectively understood but not lived concern. But for me, it is my life. It lingers even if I've taken my aspec glasses off for the day.

And it's not just me, or just aros, or even just aspecs more broadly. There are plenty of allos who grapple with this fear as well, whether it's because they're divorced or chronically anxious or just burned by love.

It's almost as if we would all benefit from a society that not just tolerates but encourages robust platonic bonds and support systems.

Huh. Weird.

In an increasingly well-connected and well-documented world, the idea that platonic friendships sit firmly in a second tier of relationships has only become more and more fixed in our social structure. Says Cohen when discussing the work of the aforementioned Professor Elizabeth Brake, "Because friendship is outside the realm of legal protection, the law perpetuates the norm that friendships are less valuable than romantic relationships." When dealing with death, finances, or property, for example, there are far more hoops to jump through if you and the person with whom you wish to share these things are not bound by either blood or a legally recognized marriage. This creates a self-fulfilling prophecy, a vicious cycle wherein platonic partnerships are less valued because they have no legal standing, and there is little push for legal recognition because they carry less social value.

Some might argue that two people in a platonic partnership could simply get legally married anyway (assuming the marriage is legal where they live)—problem solved. But it's not so simple. In the United States, at least, the courts have the right to deem a marriage that isn't romantic–sexual in nature as a "sham marriage" and subsequently remove those very same benefits that the marriage provided them in the first place.[3] If the married pair can convince a court that their union wasn't made for fraudulent purposes, this can be avoided. But given that our society doesn't place the same value on intimate platonic relationships as it does on romantic–sexual ones, the genuine nature of a platonic partnership can be difficult to "prove." The self-fulfilling prophecy fulfills itself again.

To be clear, we don't mean to argue that giving two-person platonic partnerships stronger legal standing will solve all of our problems. There is, in fact, very little dialogue on what such a thing might look like, much less the impact it would have. Moreover, there is reason to believe that *Obergefell v. Hodges*, the American court case whose ruling legalized same-sex marriage on a federal level in 2015—while an incredible step forward in its own right—may have actually harmed the broader queer cause in other ways. That is, the approach queer activists took in this case was something along the lines of, "Dearest straights, us gays are just like you! We have committed, monogamous, romantic–sexual relationships! We raise good, God-fearing American children! Therefore, we are the same as the straights and should be treated as such!" In doing so, our society's traditional allonormative and amatonormative take on partnership was only further reinforced. Two steps forward, one step back.

We got something incredible out of *Obergefell* (and we surely don't intend to diminish that with our sarcasm), yet the structural integrity of the status quo remains firmly intact.

The aspec lens, of course, requires a complete dismantling of that status quo. How, then, can we apply said lens to friendship?

For those who wish to live their life through the aspec lens and treat their platonic friendships accordingly, there is no roadmap. In fact, the field is wide open—as Cohen notes, "Intimate friendships don't come with shared social scripts that lay out what they should look like or how they should progress." Luckily for those who, like us, find that prospect actually rather daunting, the aspec community has put a fair amount of thought into this topic, and the application thereof is by no means limited to those who identify under the aspec umbrella.

This can be as simple as creating language around platonic relationships: a *squish*, for example, as the equivalent of a friend crush. On the other hand, it can also be a more literal queering of the status quo.

For some, the way to do this is by embracing *relationship anarchy*, a term first coined by Andie Nordgren in 2006.[4] The term itself may sound extreme, but the concept is rather innocuous and, if you're this far into the chapter, surely already familiar to you: relationship anarchy simply means rejecting the ranking and comparing of relationships. Nordgren challenges the idea that love is a limited resource, and emphasizes an anti-hierarchical, non-normative approach. "One person in your life does not need to be named primary for the relationship to be real," she says, reinforcing her prior assertion that no one relationship can diminish the strength of another. "Each relationship is independent, and a relationship between autonomous individuals."

The concept of relationship anarchy is broad and can extend far beyond the decentering of romantic–sexual partnerships into the realms of polyamory, community-building, and a lack of state control. It is, after all, called anarchy for a reason. But the concept of anarchy—not in the literal sense of throwing bricks and burning buildings, but in the more metaphorical sense—actually has quite a lot in common with the aspec lens.

Another approach to the queering of the status quo comes from David Jay, the founder of the Asexual Visibility and Education Network (AVEN) and a man who is sometimes lovingly referred to as the "father of modern asexuality." In a talk circa 2015, he discussed sitting down with a friend of his to talk about their relationship and intentionality.[5] His relationship with said friend was completely platonic and always had been, but as an aro ace, he was seeking the kind of human connection that was talked about, celebrated, and prioritized in the way that romantic–sexual relationships so often are.

The structure of this conversation was simple: David and his friend talked about what in their relationship was working and how they wanted to build on it. For aspecs and allos alike, having such a conversation regarding a completely platonic relationship may feel a bit odd. But the reality is that this type of conversation is by no means unprecedented in our society; it's simply reserved for romantic–sexual partnerships. These types of conversations are had constantly between people in romantic-sexual relationships who are seeking to define their relationship in one way or another: whether that means becoming "official" and exclusive, discussing marriage, considering long-distance, or something else.

The resulting conversation, Jay says, completely changed the trajectory of their relationship. The nature of this relationship between him and his friend didn't change, but having a formal discussion about it, making sure they were on the same page about the importance of it and the time they wanted to dedicate to it, was transformational. It allowed the relationship to become one which was talked about, celebrated, and prioritized—by the two of them, at the very least. After the success of this first endeavor, Jay would continue to have these conversations about intentionality with other friends as the years passed by. (In fact, we'll share another intentional discussion Jay had with friends in a later chapter.)

Unfortunately, not all allos value or even approve of bringing intentionality into platonic relationships and thus allowing them to exist on the same plane as romantic–sexual connections. A few years back, a post from the "Am I the Asshole" subreddit went a bit viral in the aspec corners of social media—the original poster, Reddit user Impressive-Jaguar, had asked if she was an asshole for always putting her single best friends before her married ones.[6] She described how she and her two friends had bought adjacent properties, knocked down the existing fence, and created something of a communal living space between them. They each had their own home for when they wanted to be alone, but they also shared everything from a greenhouse and various pets to Netflix and Amazon Prime accounts. Impressive-Jaguar noted how convenient it was that their proximity meant they could care for each other when sick, sign off on each other's package deliveries, and interface with one another's repair people if one couldn't be home for the repair.

She then went on to explain that her married friends had begun to grow annoyed with her habit of checking with these two close friends to make sure she didn't have any conflicting plans before making arrangements with others. Impressive-Jaguar didn't understand this frustration, likening it to her married friends asking the very same of their spouses before making plans with her—something they routinely did. She noted that she never begrudged her married friends for canceling plans because their spouse was sick, but they reacted poorly to her doing the same for her two friends. "I essentially live with and share most of my life with [these friends]," she argued, so why should it not be acceptable for her to prioritize them?

Not only did the people of Reddit find that Impressive-Jaguar was overwhelmingly *not* the asshole, but many in the aspec community expressed an interest in her way of life. Online, people of all identities joked that living like this would be "the dream," but for many aspecs, it wasn't a joke at all. Several people noted that this relationship she had with her two friends seemed like an almost-textbook queerplatonic relationship, a type of more-established platonic partnership certainly not limited to aspecs but much more prevalent in our community than others (a concept which we will discuss in more detail in the next chapter).

In her post, Impressive-Jaguar gave no indication that she might be aspec; in fact, at one point she referred to herself as "chronically single," implying that if given the choice, she might not be. Yet the life she had built was profoundly attractive to a great many aspecs, and the conflict she was facing because of her lifestyle was based in the very same garden-variety amatonormativity that aspecs face daily.

So, what does this all mean for the aspec lens? We don't necessarily expect all of our readers to go full David Jay, sitting down with all their friends to discuss intentionality. We certainly don't expect you to go out and buy land with a small group of your closest friends and go in on a shared coop of chickens (although if you do, please send us pictures).

In this context, applying the aspec lens to your friendships is really about self-awareness. Think about the relationships you prioritize: why do you prioritize them? Do you surround yourself with people who value each of their relationships on their own merit, or do you surround yourself with people whose relationships are tiered based on type? It's impossible to not be around *anyone* who automatically favors romantic–sexual relationships, because that's just the world we live in, but are you challenging those in your life who do?

One last time, we'd like to emphasize that we are not anti-romantic–sexual relationships—Kayla is literally in one! For some individuals, viewing the world through the aspec lens might mean deprioritizing their romantic–sexual relationships, but those individuals are likely in the minority. What the aspec lens asks us to do is not necessarily to deprioritize, but to decenter. To stop defaulting to whatever society tells us is most important and start making those decisions for ourselves. If the conclusion you come to at any given time is that your romantic–sexual partnership is the current priority in your life, as society suggests it ought to be, then that's totally fine. But what's important is that you came to that conclusion yourself.

Worth mentioning, however, is that in discussing the prioritization of platonic relationships, the focus is always more so on the bond that results rather than the way these relationships form. We would be remiss not to address that the way said relationships are formed is, like everything else, not universal.

The label of aplatonic is a lesser-known label even within the aspec community, but in the same vein as asexual and aromantic, it describes a person who experiences little to no platonic attraction. As a culture, we don't often think about platonic connections in the sense of attraction. Being drawn to someone platonically may feel less like a sustained or recurring feeling than romantic or sexual attraction—one and done. Whether this is the inherent nature of platonic attraction, merely a result of our society's preference towards the romantic–sexual attraction it knows and values best, or a little bit of both, it remains true that most people do experience platonic attraction, even if they're not fully aware of it.

Many of us have at one point or another experienced a phenomenon which we briefly touched upon above: a "friend crush," aka a *squish*. Someone who, although we don't necessarily want to date them or have sex with them, we nonetheless want to get close to. Someone who we like, not just in a passive, "yeah, they're cool" kind of way, but in a "I feel compelled to actively seek out a relationship with this person and will be upset if it doesn't work out" kind of way. This is that platonic attraction of which we speak, and which aplatonic folks either never or rarely experience.

Just as ace folks can have sex and aro folks can engage in what any outsider would describe as romance, it's not as though aplatonic folks are incapable of forming platonic relationships or close bonds in general. The label simply means that they don't experience that platonic attraction that so many others take for granted.

Some aplatonic folks, then, are frustrated with the way platonic relationships are so often emphasized and idolized in aspec spaces. It might be equated to the same faults that we identified in the American approach to legalizing same-sex marriage—except instead of saying, "We're just like you! We have relationships and sex, too!" it's saying, "We're just like you! We experience squishes too!" Instead of the emphasis being on the fact that the system is based on a foundational misunderstanding of what should be, the emphasis is placed on reassuring others that *don't worry, we may do things a little differently, but we're still normal.*

The perspective we gain from the aspec lens, of course, comes not just from ace and aro identities, but from everything under the aspec umbrella. It's important that we make space in the community for aplatonic folks and consider their needs and perspectives as we turn our purple-colored glasses to our own community as well.

At the same time, however, for many aspecs—aplatonic or not—celebrating platonic bonds and platonic friendships is a crucial aspect of their identity. A large portion of the aspec community shares the sentiments of American novelist Hanya Yanagihara, who says, "Friendship is the most underrated relationship in our lives ... It remains the one relation not bound by law, blood, or money—but an unspoken agreement of love."[7] Just as sex and romance only have power (maybe too much power) because we give it to them, the same can be said here. Platonic bonds have power because we give them power—and we can actively choose to make them more or less powerful in our lives. The more we feed the dragon, the stronger it grows.

One of the defining characteristics of the human race is that we are social pack animals. We create community not just by blood, but also by choice—it's called a support *system* for a reason. It's not an exaggeration to say that without platonic relationships, humanity would not be where it is today. This is true on a large scale: if every farmer at the start of the agricultural revolution simply refused to share their crops with anyone but their romantic–sexual partner and their offspring, communities would not have formed as they did, and the domino effect might have taken our species in an entirely different direction. But this is also true on a small scale: who would you be if, after a break up or a divorce or the death of a partner, you had no one to go to to hold your hand and no shoulder to cry on? To the modern human, an existence devoid of platonic friendship would be not just isolating, but also completely unrecognizable. The world as we know it is built upon a foundation of platonic love, support, and care, and always has been.

The aspec lens merely asks that we start acting like it.

Scan this QR code or click on the link below to access a bonus podcast episode about the making of this chapter.

https://www.soundsfakepod.com/sounds-book-but-okay-friendship

CHAPTER 4

Romance and Partnerships

Okay, so we've now firmly established that romantic-sexual relationships are not inherently superior to platonic ones. And as we learn from aromanticism more broadly, romantic attraction is not even necessary for all people. But the fact remains that many people do still experience this attraction and/or want to pursue romantic relationships, so what can the aspec lens teach us about how we might approach them differently?

As we hinted at in the previous chapter, relationships that are both sexual and romantic in nature are not the only kind of partnerships people can take part in. While some aspecs, like Sarah, might find themselves content in their singleness, others want one or more people with whom they can more formally partner to share their lives. And some aspecs may not necessarily be looking for a partnership at all, but—as is often said of romantic-sexual relationships—the right one lands in their lap when they least expect it.

Moreover, aspecs aren't limited to certain types of supposedly "aspec-friendly" relationships such as friendships or queerplatonic relationships (which we'll get to shortly), just as allos aren't limited to traditional romantic–sexual relationships. When it comes to types of partnerships, the sky is truly the limit. But for the sake of ease, let's start somewhere familiar.

If you're reading this book, you probably already know this, but just in case you don't, let's begin with a basic fact: yes, asexual people can be and are in romantic relationships. We'll even take it a step further: aromantic people can be and are in romantic relationships. Does this seem counterintuitive? Maybe. But in the end, romantic relationships are simply a structure that is a combination of normative activities and practices. You go on dates, maybe you hold hands, you give gifts. Do any of these activities require romantic attraction? Or sexual attraction, for that matter? Not at all. In the end, they're just activities that society has deeply intertwined with certain feelings and attractions.

This isn't to say that aspec people are always able to date or form partnerships with ease or in the same way allo people do. Because there are such strict norms around relationships, and because aspec identities are so unknown, entering a partnership with an allo person, or even just casual dating, can have a unique set of challenges. Dating becomes not only telling a person about yourself, but telling them, and often teaching them, about your sexuality and/or romantic orientation.

Kayla

When I started dating my current partner Dean, I was out as demisexual. It had been about a year since the events outlined in Chapter 2, and I was much more confident in my sexuality. I opened every podcast episode with "and me, a demi-straight girl,"[a] shared the show on social media, and talked about it in my day-to-day life. Even so, I wasn't sure that Dean actually knew I was demisexual. We knew each other casually through being on the Quidditch team together (yes, myself, Dean, *and* Sarah all did Quidditch in college) but it wasn't like we were close friends before we started talking and then dating.

With my online dating profiles, it had been easy. I just put "demisexual" in my bio and called it a day. I was expecting a bit of pushback or aphobia for that but surprisingly, none came. Perhaps that was just yet another privilege of living in a liberal college bubble. Either way, it was much more difficult when dating in person. What was I supposed to say? "Uhm by the way, I'm not sure if you listen to my podcast but I am demisexual, and here's what that means." It just felt so awkward, both to have to educate him on the asexual spectrum but also to admit I had a podcast.

Luckily, but unluckily at the same time, I never had to have this conversation with him myself. Shortly after we started dating, at some random party, a mutual friend of ours was talking to Dean about our relationship. The friend listened to the podcast religiously, so they knew very well that I was demisexual. At some point, they asked Dean, "You know she's demisexual, right?" On the bright side, it turns out Dean did know, so that was a plus.

When Dean told me about this conversation, I was crushed. Though our friend hadn't meant for the comment to be malicious, I took it as an attack. I worried that our friend's comment had been meant as a sort of warning, as them saying, "Are you

---

a   Now, only a year after writing this, I open with "and me, a bi demisexual girl." See, identities change!

sure you want to date her? You know she's demisexual, so she won't put out right away."

After hearing from Dean, I speed-walked back from the library and, in very dramatic fashion, burst into Sarah's room sobbing. Though I obviously knew that I was out to the world as demisexual, that thousands of strangers listened to me talk about my orientation every week, I had never truly considered that people I *knew* would have an interest in or talk about my sexuality when I wasn't even there. It should have been obvious, I suppose, but it terrified me. It shook that newfound confidence that I felt I had in my sexuality.

Sarah, though bewildered and not the most skilled at handling outbursts of emotions, calmed me down and told me everything would be fine. And she was right. Dean already knew that I was demisexual and didn't care. Looking back now, I realize that the main driver of my emotions about the situation was insecurity and fear. I was so worried that when Dean found out I was demisexual, he wouldn't want to date me anymore or that he would judge me or say something rude. I was so worried that my sexuality, something I had no control over, would get in the way of me having the relationship I wanted.

Aside from potentially having to give your partner or date an entire TED Talk on the aspectrum, one of the most difficult parts about dating as an aspec person is that same fear and anxiety that Kayla felt. As PJ put it:

I need someone that wholeheartedly understands and supports

that I am not at all interested in sex. Being sex-repulsed, it's terrifying to think about being rejected for something I have no control over. It's terrifying to think about being rejected for something I wish I wanted. (PJ S.—they/them—asexual, biromantic)

Of course, it is completely valid for people to need sex in their relationships, but it doesn't make it any easier to cope with being rejected because of your sexuality or level of interest in sex. For some, the possibility of this rejection hinders their partnerships more than the rejection itself.

I also always have the worry in the back of my mind (even when I'm dating someone who says they are cool with it) that people will not be okay with my sexuality in the long run, whether that's in wanting more sexual experiences or in them feeling insecure about the fact that I don't find them sexually attractive. My own fears probably ruin more chances than my asexuality actually would but it's hard to convince myself. (Mariah—she/her—greysexual, panromantic)

While in a relationship, it's hard to decide when and how to tell someone about your sexuality (a problem that Kayla was able to ungracefully sidestep, but that many aspecs are forced to grapple with). Do you tell them on the first date and risk them no longer wanting to see you? Do you wait until you've gotten to know each other a bit better only to feel like you've been keeping a secret the entire time? Unfortunately, we don't have a clear answer for you or a sage piece of wisdom. As with all things relationship-related, you have to do what feels right (and safe) for you.

Despite these difficulties, dating as an aspec person is not all bad. In fact, there are many, many unique positives. As we discussed in Chapter 2, by having to question themselves and society so deeply, aspec people often know themselves incredibly well. Because of this, many aspecs know exactly what their boundaries are in terms of sex and romance and have a pretty good idea of what they want in a relationship and what they are able to give.

We will stop to note that understanding these preferences does take time, so don't feel discouraged if you aren't there yet. Unfortunately, coming to terms with your asexuality and/or aromanticism does not come with a free lifetime supply of perfect awareness of your boundaries. If only it were that easy. Instead, it comes from trial and error and deep introspection.

This introspection leads us aspecs not only to think deeply and question everything about ourselves but also question the ways we relate to other people and the world around us. While allos may be content to assume that they will end up with a partner that they are compatible with when it comes to emotional, physical, and other boundaries, aspecs are painfully aware that this is not always the case. This makes the topic of romantic relationships and how to make them work a particularly popular one in the aspec community. Though from the outside people may assume that aspecs have no care for romance or partnerships, this could not be further from the truth.

In fact, when we were initially approached to write this book, our editor pitched it to us as a book solely about asexual relationships. When we were panelists at an asexuality conference, the panel Kayla spoke on about dating as an aspec person was one of the most popular. Because aspecs have non-normative identities and non-normative preferences and needs, we are forced to spend more time thinking about how to make our relationships work than anyone else.

Still don't believe us? Think about this: your average, norm-abiding person has a very clear path to forming and maintaining a "successful" and socially acceptable relationship. This path is something that Amy Gahran refers to as "the relationship escalator" in her book *Stepping off the Relationship Escalator: Uncommon Love and Life*. Gahran describes the relationship escalator like this:

> two (and only two) people progress from initial attraction and dating, to becoming sexually and romantically involved and exclusive, to adopting a shared identity as a couple, to moving in together and otherwise merging their lives—all the way up to marriage and kids, 'til death do you part.[8]

Why is it a relationship escalator, you ask? Rather than some relationship stairs or a nice steep relationship hill? Well, across the Western world, the escalator is the unspoken standard for relationships. It is how we judge whether a relationship is good and healthy. And because this model is so ingrained in our culture and in our minds, relationships that follow it are inherently supported more and take less work, just like taking an escalator is quicker and lower effort than taking the stairs or climbing a hill.[9]

When you think about relationships that include one or more aspec people, you can see how the relationship escalator starts to crumble or become irrelevant. The relationship escalator assumes and necessitates sex, something that not all aspec relationships have. And for aspec partnerships that do include sex, sexual and/or romantic attraction may not exist or may be formed in a unique way. Even aspec relationships that seem to ride the relationship escalator from the outside may be quite complex and different when you look closer. As Gahran says, "simply by having intimate relationships at all, on their own terms, asexual people are taking a big step off the Relationship Escalator."[10]

So, where does this leave aspecs who are interested in forming partnerships? Where do we go from here? Well, one option is to ride the escalator, or an approximate version of the escalator, with a fellow aspec or with an allo person. Aspecs are fully capable of forming traditional, monogamous, committed relationships; it may just come with some unique challenges, especially if it is an allo/aspec relationship. In the end, these relationships come down to two things that are imperative to all relationships: communication and compromise (the kind that goes both ways).

In relationships across the board, not just aspec relationships, people's goals, preferences, sex drives, and/or love languages might differ. While these differences may be more pronounced in allo/aspec relationships, they are not necessarily insurmountable. Though it may be uncomfortable to discuss boundaries or whether you're sex-averse or sex-favorable early in a relationship, it makes for a better partnership in the end.

Compromise is, of course, a necessary component of all relationships, no matter their type, but this can be especially difficult when it comes to things like sex. Compromises on the amount or type of sex a couple has aren't impossible, but for some, it just doesn't work.

> It also is difficult because sexual "compromise" is normalized, wherein a person loses their ability to reject the partner the longer the relationship goes because it's not satisfying their needs. (Phoebe Langley—she/they—bisexual[b])

---

b   You may have noticed that our respondent Phoebe does not identify on the aspectrum. While at the time of writing their quote they did identify as asexual, they no longer do. We'll return to Phoebe later on to hear more about their journey to figuring out their identity as an allosexual, alloromantic, and bisexual trans woman.

Unfortunately, the word which always comes to mind when I think of dating as an asexual person is "compromise." (Jen Liang —she/her—asexual, aromantic)

For those not inclined to take an escalator ride, there are many more non-traditional options. The aspec lens and relationship anarchy teach us that there is so much outside of the traditional relationship escalator if we are only willing to put in a bit of work and customize our partnerships to be exactly what we need.

Not all of these options have fancy names such as the escalator, of course. It would be impossible to give a name to every customized, non-normative relationship that every partnership comes up with. But there are a few that have become so ingrained in aspec and queer culture that they have earned formal titles.

The first of these, being the apple of the aspec community's eye, is the queerplatonic relationship (QPR). Given its name, you may feel that it's counterintuitive for us to be discussing QPRs here, rather than in Chapter 3. But that's the beautiful thing about QPRs—they're fluid, they're customizable, and they can be any kind of partnership you want them to be.

Ideally, we'd be able to give you a hard and fast definition of QPRs, one that we could slap in the Dictionary and that everyone, aspec and allo alike, could agree upon. Unfortunately, that is impossible. While the vagueness of QPRs is their shining quality, it does make it a bit difficult to define and describe in a book. But for you, we will try anyway.

In general terms, a queerplatonic relationship is a committed partnership that is based in friendship (as its title would suggest). Even so, QPRs are not necessarily devoid of all romantic and sexual acts or attractions. They could involve romance and sex, but they don't have to—that's where the fluidity comes in.

The addition of sex and/or romance may make a QPR look like a typical relationship from the outside, but there is one key difference between QPRs and normative romantic–sexual relationships: choice. In typical escalator relationships, sex and romance are not just expected, but almost required. But for people in QPRs, you start with a platonic bond and add from there.

If the infinite number of normative sexual and romantic acts and attractions were a grocery store, escalator couples would be handed a shopping list by the all-powerful society that includes one of everything. Without thinking, and without knowing if they do really want to purchase everything, they would move forward and go on a little shopping spree.[c] Queerplatonic partners, on the other hand, give a firm "no thank you" to society and spend time creating their own shopping list, carefully considering all of the options available (including non-normative ones), reflecting on their boundaries and interests, and deciding if they even want to go to the store at all.

And say they don't go shopping—say these partners elect to add no romance or sex to their partnership and instead to stay purely platonic. Would that not just be a friendship? Why give it a special name? What makes a QPR different from an average friendship is the level of commitment involved. With a typical friend, you may not sit down with them to discuss your combined life goals, you might not merge your finances or build a shared life together. Often, QPRs will have the same type of formal commitment and planning that a romantic–sexual relationship would have.

For aspec folks, it is the very vagueness that makes it so hard

---

c   This obviously isn't to say that all traditional romantic–sexual relationships are the same or that they lack customized and non-normative options; we're simply talking in broad strokes about the "ideal" escalator relationship in the eyes of society.

to define, the grocery shopping of it all, that makes it so attractive. With their needs so often left out of the traditional path of the escalator relationship, aspecs are able to use the philosophy of QPRs to get what they truly need from their partnerships.

> I guess that's exactly what I like. Not having a checklist of what your relationship *must* be like (like, socially, romantic relationships do). Not having to conform to a "standard" or a "norm," and instead being able to talk about it with your partner and decide what your relationship means to you, what it involves, and so on. (Nic—he/they—asexual, lesbian-oriented)

> It is a blank canvas that all partners can help paint together, creating something that is unique to them and their relationship. (Amber—she/they—asexual, aromantic, queer)

> You really get to design the relationship from the ground up, cherry-picking the elements of friendship and romance you want, and leaving the rest behind. (Max—they/them—demisexual, demiromantic)

We should also reiterate that the nebulous definition we have provided here is not the definitive definition, nor should it be. While we posited that QPRs often involve long-term commitment, for example, this doesn't have to be true for everyone.

> I don't actually think that QPRs need to plan their lives around each other as is commonly described by other members of the community. I think long term that may happen in a QPR, but that especially for younger people or newer relationships, expecting to plan your life around this other person may be too much pressure. (Anneke—she/her—asexual, aromantic)

We understand that with such a vague definition laid in front of you, you may still be lacking a clear picture of what it truly is to be in a QPR. And while neither of us can provide personal anecdotes about being in a QPR, we can share a few from our respondents.

> I've been in a QPR with an amazing partner for eleven years as of the time I'm writing this. What interests me is the physical and emotional intimacy and commitment that I just don't get in any of my other relationships. With my partner, I feel complete freedom to be myself and hide nothing from him. My QPR is everything I could ever want in a relationship without the expectation of romance or sex. (Ayana—they/them—asexual, aromantic)

> I have been in a QPR with my wonderful partner for a while. We are long distance and polyam. It is great for me, I don't feel pressure to talk to them all the time or to be on the relationship escalator.
>
> For us it's about having someone to cuddle, do kink things with, do dates sometimes …
>
> I am really grateful to have someone like them because sex isn't expected. Although I am kinky, I am sex averse, I want to keep that for just me thanks very much, so having deep friendships which can be intimate but not sexual or overly romantic is amazing! (Frances—xe/xem—asexual, aromantic)

Though QPRs are the perfect solution for many aspecs seeking partnerships or formal companionship, there is one area in which they are lacking: legal protection. Just as we mentioned in the previous chapter, marrying a platonic partner is not as easy as it may seem. Ideally, marriage would not be necessary at all to receive the legal and financial benefits of a formal partnership, but unfortunately this is the position society has put us in.

While alternative relationships offer many benefits to queer folks, legal difficulties will always linger in the background, and nowhere is that more true than in polyamorous relationships. While polyamory is by no means specific to the aspec community, it can provide elegant solutions to some of the difficulties that aspecs often face while dating and forming relationships. When it comes to forming a partnership where sexual incompatibility may be an issue, some aspecs find that opening their relationships can ease some of that burden.

> I identify as polyamorous. My partner doesn't pressure me to have sex (or he wouldn't be my partner). Even so, it's helpful when we are discussing our relationship for both of us to know that I don't have to fulfill his every need. If he wants more sex, he can find another partner. (Jesslyn/JJ—all—asexual, biromantic)

Others, like Frances, have simply found that the ideals and tenets of the polyamorous community fit well with asexuality and aromanticism.

> It's lovely that there are spaces like the polyam community where there is less of that [set expectations] and more discussions about how the people involved want relationships to look and feel. (Frances—xe/xem—asexual, aromantic)

And it makes sense that this match of ideals would occur. Both the aspec lens and the polyamorous lens are strongly influenced by relationship anarchy and the idea that one person does not need to fulfill every single need a person possesses.

Lately I just discovered that I might be interested in a polyamorous relationship because as someone who is aspec and uses the split attraction model, I realized that my attractions are oftentimes not aligned with one another. As a result I might feel a deep connection that includes aesthetic, sensual and sexual attraction towards one person and another deep connection that includes platonic, sensual and alterous attraction[d] towards another person. (Astrini Adisoma—she/her—asexual/greysexual, aromantic)

I don't know whether this a unique experience due to the fact that I am aspec, but I personally found it easy to find different needs met by different partners much in the same way I already did with friends and having different friends to meet to talk about and do different things. (Eliott Scott Simpson—he/they—asexual, panromantic)

Much like QPRs, polyamorous relationships are incredibly customizable and look different for every person. Nevertheless, here is just one example of what a polyamorous setup can look like:

I have benefitted greatly from the open, polyamorous setup that I currently have—it is incredibly freeing to be in a relationship that fulfills me romantically without feeling the guilt/obligation/sadness of being unable to fulfill my partners' sexual desires. I love to participate in a romantic evening with my partners and then set up the bedroom for them to have a special time together while I go play video games or read or whatever—the

---

d   Alterous attraction defines the desire to be emotionally close to someone in a way that is not wholly romantic nor platonic, but instead somewhere in the middle.

feeling of compersion is incredible and the hugs afterwards are my favorite. I feel included in the intimacy and emotional closeness without needing to get involved in sex. (Anita—she/her—asexual, panromantic)

Though polyamory and aspec identities may mesh well for some, that does not mean that it's for everyone. While one of the perks of polyamory may be that it takes the pressure off an aspec person to be sexual and/or romantic with their partner, this should by no means be the only reason to enter into a polyamorous relationship.

I was in a theoretically open relationship. It helped, even in theory, because my partner was able to find other people to satisfy their sexual desires. It helped me a lot because I had far less pressure to fulfill that. Even though they never found another partner, it made it so I could be far more comfortable not providing that to them. It was now fully their responsibility.

The difficulty there is that polyamory can be one-sided when it's motivated that way. I ended up finding another potential partner sheerly out of luck and it was difficult for my current partner to handle. (Phoebe Langley—she/they—bisexual)

It goes without saying that polyamorous partnerships, like any other partnership, should be entered into for the right reasons. Polyamory can and does help a lot of partnerships overcome sexual or romantic incompatibility, but this should not come at the cost of the rest of the relationship. We heard from countless survey respondents that they feared it might be necessary to enter into a polyamorous relationship just to keep their partnership alive, or just to start one in the first place.

As we have stated before, compromise is necessary for every

relationship. But a compromise that makes you uncomfortable is never worth it. A partnership that is entered into on terms that are not comfortable for every party is doomed from the start. Though polyamory may "save" your relationship in the short term, if you enter into it because of necessity rather than desire, your relationship has not truly been saved.

This same idea and warning pertains to QPRs, as well as traditional romantic–sexual relationships. In a similar fashion, many respondents showed interest in entering a QPR not necessarily because of the philosophy behind the relationship structure, but because being in a QPR would ward off loneliness. Many shared Sarah's same concerns that their allo friends would pair off and leave them behind. They reasoned that if they had a QPR, a partner of their own, they wouldn't be so lonely.

Upon first glance, this may seem sad, desperate even. But we encourage you to recall that this is an incredibly common mindset for aspecs and allos alike. How many romantic–sexual relationships have you watched form before your very eyes simply because the members didn't want to "die alone"? How many dates have you seen your friends go on simply because they were bored or lonely or sick of being single?

We understand that we have just spent an entire chapter detailing different ways aspecs can navigate relationships, but we urge you to remember that entering into a partnership is *not* necessary. Though society urges us to couple off, though the world is built for pairs, the option to remain single is always available. Of course, like everything else in this book, this is easier said than done. Unfortunately, couple privilege and amatonormativity both exist and even thrive in our society, but that doesn't make a single lifestyle impossible. As always, the only right answer is the one that's right for you, and for better or for worse, you are the only one who can decide what that is.

Aspec or otherwise, the best thing you can do for yourself, and others, is to deeply analyze what you do and don't want in a partnership. If at the end of the day you come to the conclusion that you are interested in a relationship-escalator-type partnership, that's completely fine. There is no shame in going down this route as long as you choose it freely, rather than as a default.

The myriad of different approaches aspecs take to romance specifically and partnerships more broadly only go to prove the point we made at the beginning of this chapter as it pertains to partnerships: the sky's the limit. The more allos that join us in donning our aspec glasses and actively choosing to buck the status quo, the more we add to the infinite and ever-expanding list of how human partnerships can take shape, and the more our culture can move away from the restrictive, prescriptive relationship escalator.

Scan this QR code or click on the link below to access a bonus podcast episode about the making of this chapter.

https://www.soundsfakepod.com/sounds-book-but-okay-romance-and-partnerships

CHAPTER 5

Sex

A taboo and a necessity, simultaneously vilified and wor-shipped, sex is an enigma, and in no place is this more true than in the aspec community. When reading about asexuality in mass media, you typically see two things. First, articles with flashy titles like "No sex please!" or "Meet the group who's saying no to sex." And then, the well-meaning yet slightly misguided retort: "Asexual people *do* still have sex!"

It's true. Some asexual people (many, in fact) do have sex for a variety of reasons that we'll get into later. But it's that word *still* that's a bit troubling. Saying *still* hedges the assertion, implying that the person is saying, "No, no I swear, asexual people are normal. We have sex just like you!"

It's a double-edged sword. When you're aspec, it can be hard to gain acceptance, to convince people that you are real, valid, healthy even. It's tempting to say *still*, to insist that we're just like everyone else. But in the best way possible, we aren't. Because even if you're an aspec person who has sex, you're probably both doing it and thinking about it a lot differently than the allo people in your life.

When people learn that many asexual people do have sex, they are often shocked. "How?" they ask. "How is it possible to have sex without sexual attraction?" The first step to understanding this is detaching sexual *attraction* from sexual *action*. At first glance, these may seem inherently linked, just like romantic activities and romantic feelings seem linked. To some, it may seem incomprehensible or even impossible to take part in a sexual act without feeling that attraction. And because society tells us that they must be linked, it is difficult to differentiate them, even for aspec folks. We have received countless messages from aspec people over the years questioning if they are actually aspec because they enjoy sex so much. But when we put on our aspec glasses and look past the taboos and the many false ideas that the world has hammered into our subconscious, we find that the very same society that is in such disbelief over the actions of aspecs might actually be a bit hypocritical (shocking, we know).

What's interesting is that even for allo folks, sexual attraction is not always the main driver of sex. It is simply impossible that every drunken hook up that ever was, every late-night "you up?" ever sent, has been accompanied by a strong feeling of sexual attraction. What we're made to believe, though, is that these situations are the exception, not the rule. Society tells us that the purest and most acceptable form of sex is sex that is accompanied by strong feelings of not only sexual, but also romantic, attraction. It's the difference between the taboo "sex" and the romantic and idyllic "making love." One is deemed for sluts and players, the other for your God-fearing grandparents.[a]

For asexual folks, sex without sexual attraction is not just an outlier, it's the norm (excluding, of course, those demisexual and greysexual folks who do develop feelings of sexual attraction

---

[a] Our apologies for making you think about your grandparents having sex. Our apologies, as well, to any self-identified slutty grandparents who feel misrepresented by our words.

under certain circumstances and on certain occasions). Without the assistance or direction of that trusty attraction, asexuals who have an interest in sex are left to decide when to have sex, why to have sex, and who to have sex with on their own—with, of course, the help of their libido.

> Personally, I am a sexual being in that I do have a libido. However, since I am asexual, I don't have any specific type of person that I want to act on those urges with. My sex drive isn't "directed" at anyone, it just exists. It's kinda like a treadmill, I can run to let off some steam, but I'm not actually "going" anywhere, if that makes sense. (Sunny—she/they—asexual, aromantic)

We are then left with the question on everyone's lips: without sexual attraction, without that "direction," why do asexuals have sex? In the end, it can be for the same reasons that anyone else might.

> I have sex because I see it as more of a romantic activity than a sexual activity. I find it helps build a connection and trust. (Paddy—he/him—asexual)

> From sex, I like how it feels for sure, but also it's like an enjoyable activity to do with people I'm close to. I like the physical affection that often comes with it, plus it's a great time to play with kinks. And I genuinely enjoy making the other person happy as well! Oh, also, I have a high libido, and while taking care of that alone is fine, it's a lot more fun with friends! (Noelwiz—he/him—asexual, aromantic)

> What drives me to have sex is my curiosity of it and well, my sexual urges. (Omnommia—any—greysexual, aromantic)

Often times, having sex is a way to express my love and attraction to my husband. But lately my main motivation for having sex is trying to get pregnant with our second child. (Danielle Hutchison—she/her—asexual, heteroromantic)

Horniness, physical pleasure, bonding and intimacy, or good old-fashioned baby makin'—there are countless reasons for anyone, aspec or allo, to participate in sexual activities. It would be inaccurate to say, of course, that only asexual people have "reasons" for having sex and that allos simply do it without cause or motive. It does seem, however, that for asexuals, these reasons are more top of mind. Whether this is inherent to the aspec lens or comes from some outward source is the real question.

The conclusion we have come to after much deliberation and a few focus groups with our allo friends[b] (yes, we had to call some allo friends to make sure we understood the way they have sex),[c] is that the reason aspecs intellectualize sex so easily, the reason we are able to list off the motivations for why we have sex so clearly, is because we are so often asked to. This isn't to say we wouldn't have thought about these things on our own—we certainly do by nature of thinking and questioning our sexualities so deeply—but there is certainly something to be said for the outside pressure we receive to explain ourselves.

When we called our allo friends, they too were able to tell us why they had sex (horniness, stress relief, a spur of the moment feeling, etc.). Prying these answers from them was not necessarily

---

b   It should be noted that we did not hold actual, scientific focus groups. Rather, we called a few friends via Snapchat from a small RV in Austin, Texas. We asked the chickens who lived outside of the RV to participate in the group but unfortunately, they declined.

c   Special thanks to Artemis, Jared, Max, and Perry for their contributions. No thanks to the chickens.

easy, however. It took several tries and different phrasings of our question for them to finally understand what we were asking. In the end, they revealed that the reasons they have sex aren't something they think about often, and that no one had ever asked them why they did it. For aspecs, this is unfortunately not the case. As we already noted, allos are often shocked to hear that aspecs have sex, and their first questions are often "Why?" or "How?" When giving someone the classic asexuality TED Talk, it is almost a requirement to include a segment on sex. And to prove to them that yes, it is possible to have sex, we have to list the reasons why.

Is this ideal? Of course not. As stated at the top of this chapter, it can be incredibly harmful to center sex in all conversations about aspec identities. But this forced introspection, the type of introspection that aspecs are already predisposed to, does make for a pretty powerful component of the aspec lens.

Kayla

As she instructed me to, I texted Sarah a link to The Lonely Island's "I Just Had Sex" after I had sex for the first time. She sent some exclamation points, I'm sure, and curiously asked what it felt like, if it hurt. Spoiler alert: it did. A surprise to no one, the American education system's version of "sex ed" doesn't actually prepare you to have sex. I had to text my nurse sister to ask her if bleeding was normal after your first time (it is).

Sarah then asked me a question that I wasn't expecting, a question I remember to this day. "Do you think you'll do it again?" I was taken aback at first. The thought that I wouldn't have sex again had never crossed my mind; the possibility that someone would try it once and say, "No thank you, that's not for me" was foreign to me. I told her yes because that was the truth. My first time wasn't amazing, I don't think anyone's is, but I had enjoyed it enough to get past the initial pain and awkwardness.

But her question stuck with me, as did the idea behind it. If my answer had been no, if after that first time I never wanted to have sex again, that would have been fine. Sarah, at the very least, would have accepted me.

What Sarah unintentionally taught me that day is an integral part of the aspec lens: the idea that sex does not *have* to be the be all end all, that it does not have to be centered in my world, that it's perfectly okay to take it or leave it, just like I would any other activity throughout my life.

Just as the acts of shaking hands or hugging someone are, at their core, just a physical activity, so too is sex. This may seem a rather unromantic stance—an incredibly intellectual way of looking at an act that is deemed so special, so sacred. So, if it feels like we're intellectualizing it, stripping it down, looking at it at its most basic level without all of the societally imposed glamour, it's because we are.

I get a few things out of sex. Firstly, it's a fun physical activity. Sometimes I go hiking, sometimes I have sex. Secondly, I get to make sure my partner feels loved and appreciated. (A. Murphy —they/them—asexual, demiromantic)

I often use a metaphor of food. Sex isn't my favorite food, but it's also not my least favorite food. There can be too much of a good thing and sometimes it's been a while and I miss it. (Ophelia —she/her—asexual, biromantic)

I've described this to friends in the past by comparing it to bowling—I never suggest bowling, but if someone else wants to go bowling occasionally, I'd probably go and have fun. Sometimes I definitely do not want to go bowling. I would not want to bowl every day or even every week for the rest of my life, and there are a lot of things I would want to do before I would ever consider bowling. (Kelsi Roth—she/her—asexual, biromantic)

None of this is to say that sex shouldn't be special, or that it should hold no meaning or importance to anyone, or that it should only be intellectualized. The point we are making is the same point we made about friendships and partnerships. These things, these acts, should be given meaning by *you*. Though the world seems to think that sex is one-size-fits-all or that everyone should put equal value on it, we know this to be false. In the end, sex *is* just an activity, and it is an activity that should be defined and uniquely valued by *you*.

Because sex should be given meaning by the individual, it is also the case that losing one's "virginity" is not all that society chalks it up to be. Our social order views the concept of virginity as a highly significant and monolithic matter, but as with almost all things society-related, this is not necessarily based in any known fact. Ultimately, virginity is a social construct created by those in power (read: rich, white, cis men) to shame women into keeping themselves "pure" and to bully men who show themselves as "weak" for not participating in the boys' club culture of constant sex. After all, even amongst those who value this supposed purity culture, there is no one single definition of what virginity actually is. Is it any sexual contact whatsoever? Is it only penetrative sex? Does penetrative sex only count if it's your classic, hetero "P-in-V" sex?

At the end of the day, losing one's virginity *is* important to many people. Kayla herself viewed her first time having sex as important, and there is nothing wrong with that. But just as young people should not be shamed for waiting until their late teens to have their first kiss, it should not be a point of pain to be a "virgin." As long as calling someone a virgin remains a prevalent and biting insult, the concept of virginity—and the taboos and shame surrounding it—will remain a mainstay in our cultural conversations. It is not only harmful to aspecs (whether they do or don't have sex), but also to allos (*also* whether they do or don't have sex), since we all grow up in a culture where this one singular activity is given so much weight and power.

The point of everything said above, of this whole chapter even, is not to paint aspecs as uptight insult-policers, or robots who have sex unfeelingly, or people who go through life simply checking activities and duties off of our to-do lists. In actuality, it is the opposite. Whether it is because we are forced to by nosy questioners or it is just the nature of living life through the aspec lens, aspecs put an incredible amount of care into understanding sex, contemplating what it means to each of us as individuals, and defining our own relationships to it. The aspec lens allows us to take an act like sex—which has been imbued with so much meaning by society at large—and strip it down to its parts, and rebuild it in a way that works for us. This makes many aspecs masters of metaphor and skilled labelers.

Everyone, no matter their orientation, has a certain comfort level and interest in sex. While it is easy to assume that one's orientation would "match up" with their sexual interest, we have already proven that this is not the case. Some asexuals love sex and do it daily, while some allosexuals don't really care for it. While the world seems content to let these preferences lie in silence, assuming that everyone must share the same sexual interests and that everyone will somehow be sexually compatible, the aspec lens shows us the power of naming and differentiating.

Labeling, identifying, and validating specific and nuanced experiences is a key part of the aspec lens, as evidenced by the sheer number of micro-labels the community utilizes. These labels extend beyond orientation—things like demisexuality and lithromanticism[d]—and move into the territory of sexual and romantic interest and comfort levels. While the specific names for these labels have been debated over time, our preferred spectrum[e] is as follows:

Sex-repulsed → sex-averse → sex-indifferent → sex-favorable

On one end we have sex-repulsion, where a person may feel physically ill or disgusted at just the thought of sex. Folks who are sex-repulsed have no interest in sex and are often uncomfortable consuming any sex-related media such as porn. On the other end, we have people who are sex-favorable. These are folks who are happy to have sex and enjoy doing it. And in the middle, we have folks who are sex-averse to sex-indifferent (sometimes referred to as sex-neutral)—not necessarily disgusted by sex, but not enamored with it either. While a sex-averse person would be

---

d   Lithromantic is a romantic orientation on the aromantic spectrum. Lithromantic people experience romantic attraction, but do not desire that attraction to be reciprocated.

e   For romanticism, the spectrum is structured in the same way, simply swap "sex" for "romance."

more likely to say no to sex, often being more comfortable with it as a concept than those who are sex-repulsed but still being uncomfortable with participating themselves, a sex-indifferent person may choose to participate, perhaps if their partner was interested in sex or they found themselves particularly horny one day.

Notably, a person may not stick with one label at all times. As with sexuality and orientation, the spectrum is fluid, and someone may slide up and down the line over time or in certain situations. And though these terms are heavily integrated into the aspec community and lens, they are not specific to it, or at least they shouldn't be. Everyone, whether they choose to label themselves or not, falls somewhere on this spectrum. They just may not know that there are words for it.

These labels may not feel useful to you. You may not find comfort in or garner utility from calling yourself a sex-indifferent lesbian or romance-repulsed straight person. If that's the case, no worries. We won't take any offense. The purpose of sharing this spectrum is not to indoctrinate the entire world into our system of labels, but to show the world that it's possible. It's out there.

As we grow up, we are told one cardinal "truth": that someday we are all going to crave sex and have a high libido, that we are going to experience strong sexual attraction and want to have sex with our (opposite-sex) peers. And, of course, we are then told not to do it because it's a sin or, as the coach in *Mean Girls* tells us, we'll "get pregnant and die."

This sentiment is obviously harmful to aspecs, who often grow up feeling broken because they do not feel the same way their peers supposedly do. But it is also debilitating to allos, who are led to believe that everyone experiences sexual attraction or sexual urges in the same way. We're told that everyone apparently wants to do it all the time, and so our needs are automatically compatible with anyone we might want to enter into a sexual relationship with.[f] In the movies it seems to happen so easily. Characters fall in love, or in lust, and have perfect sex with ease, without even talking about it. They seem to just instinctually agree that "Yes, we both want to have sex right now, and this is how it's going to go."

Often, we do not learn that this is a lie until we enter into our first sexual relationships. As previously stated, sexual incompatibility is not unique to mixed allo/aspec relationships. It is incredibly rare that any one person would enter into a sexual relationship and find that both their libido and their place on the sex-averse → sex-favorable spectrum would be the exact same as their partner(s). But we are never taught that this is the case. We are left to discover this ourselves and then muddle through our sexual relationships with very little direction on how to navigate this mismatch, how to discuss these issues in partnerships, or how to compromise and reconcile. As our survey respondents shared in Chapter 2, learning how to have these discussions is one of the perks that some aspecs experience after deeply questioning their identity.

Our purple-colored glasses reveal what society and what Western "sex education" wishes to keep from us: that sex is not a monolith. The aspec lens shows us that not only is it possible to have differing sexual preferences, but that it is normal and common. Though the wider world may not have caught on yet, there is language for these differences, and it can be incredibly freeing to use.

---

f It should be noted that on the whole, we're told that men are the ones who want sex all the time and that women just have to put up with their constant demand for sex. But that's a whole other can of worms that we'll open in Chapter 7.

Scan this QR code or click on the link below to access a bonus podcast episode about the making of this chapter.

https://www.soundsfakepod.com/sounds-book-but-okay-sex

CHAPTER 6

Family

From the lack of sex education to the hierarchy of platonic and romantic relationships, we have spent this book blaming the nameless, faceless "society" for all of the harmful norms that were unceremoniously dropped upon us at birth. What we have not necessarily discussed, however, is how these norms become ingrained in us in the first place. Though it often feels like it, we do not come pre-programmed with these ideas. Instead, they are taught to us, and nine times out of ten, they are taught to us by our families.

When we are young, we see the world through the eyes—the lenses—of our parent(s) or guardian(s).[a] As they teach us how to communicate, they teach us how to interact with the world. They dress us, they feed us, they control what we watch and who we talk to. In a sense, we inherit their lenses. Until we go off to school and start learning from others, they are our one source of information.

But as we age, of course, we begin customizing our lenses.

---

a   For the sake of brevity, we will utilize "parents" for the remainder of this chapter. We use the term in the broad sense, however, meaning to be inclusive of all parents, guardians, caregivers, etc.

We learn from our friends, our 11th grade English teachers, the media we consume, that perhaps there are other ways of living. And as we all know, this is when clashing can begin. Though perhaps it is slow at first, the more different our lenses become from our parents', the more difficult certain conversations become. From politics to finances, there is no shortage of topics that can turn family dinner into a battlefield. And whether you're queer or straight, aspec or allo, it remains true that relationships, dating, and sex are always in the arsenal.

Sarah

I come from a profoundly queer family.

Between me and my gay sister, my parents have a 100 percent success rate at rearing queer children. My godfather came out as gay when I was a child and is now married with a daughter; between him, multiple cousins, and my sister, I've been to just as many gay weddings as I've been to straight ones. My dad's side of the family is so gay that at every major family event, we take a photo of the "Costello Queers"—the population of which has grown and grown as the years go by. At this point, coming outs are a fairly pedestrian, standard occurrence.

The first cousin of mine to come out, though, I remember well. His coming out was rather simple—a status update on Facebook that announced he was gay. My sister and I were too young to have Facebook at the time, and neither of my parents had it either, but some family member must've tipped my mom off, because she called me and my sister into the den, where the post was pulled up on our family desktop computer. She showed it to us.

"You know what this means, right?" she asked. We said yes. "You know that this is okay, right?" We said yes. "Do you have any questions?" We said no. That was that, and we were free to go back to playing or watching TV or whatever it was that we did as preteens.

I recognize that I am incredibly privileged to have been raised in such a welcoming environment. Any child who has a family open to queerness is lucky, much less one whose parents also specifically bring up queerness with them, just to make sure that their children know where they stand.

By the time I had come to terms with my own aspec identity, I had two out cousins, an out godfather, and an out sister. I knew for a fact that my parents would be open to however I identified, that they would love me no less. Because they supported my sister so fully from the very start, I even had concrete evidence of what my coming out might look like and how our relationship might change (or not change). But in spite of this all, I also knew that coming out would not be easy.

I knew that even if my parents had heard of asexuality before, they certainly weren't familiar with the split model of attraction and wouldn't have an understanding of what it really means to be aspec. I knew that even if they were okay with the fact that I wasn't interested in a traditional romantic–sexual relationship and nuclear family unit, they would still have to completely reconceptualize what they expected my life to look like. Reconceptualize what they expected *their* lives to look like with me as their daughter—maybe they wouldn't someday be walking me down the aisle like they expected. Maybe I would never make them the grandparents they hoped to eventually be.

Meanwhile, at the time they learned I was asexual, I was thousands of miles and an ocean away on my semester-long study abroad trip in Germany. Oh, and I had recently decided to major in film and television, a career path that would almost certainly entail me moving post-graduation to sunny Los Angeles, five hours by plane and three time zones away from home. So, it was probably a lot for them to take in. (Sorry about that, y'all.)

Still, they were troupers. I'm paraphrasing here, but my mother's response was something along the lines of, "I have absolutely no idea what any of this means, but I love you and I support you!" It would take many conversations (thankfully not *too* awkward) and many resources sent before my parents would really get a good grasp on what my identity was, what it meant, or how it would impact my life. I would give the aspec TED Talk to family members many times over. Even my sister, who later admitted to having suspected that I might be aspec before I ever came out, would have plenty to learn.

My family still has questions all these years later. Hell, *I* still have questions, because the aspectrum is a seemingly infinite trove of words and concepts and love whose combined meaning cannot possibly be fully mastered by a single mortal being. But the people I love continue to try, and so do I.

I share this not to brag or boast about my personal experience, but to convey to you, dear reader, that even in the most welcoming of environments, existing as an aspec is not a walk in the park. Family is complicated. Aspec identities are woefully misunderstood, if they're understood at all. And as Kayla and I have established throughout this book, the traditional family structures around which our entire social order is based are not necessarily designed with us in mind.

God, I wish they were, but they're not.

When we came out to our families, we started in the best position possible. We are white, cis, young women who grew up in middle-class American families that, on the whole, are liberal and accepting in their views. And yet, as Sarah states, being aspec is not a walk in the park for anyone. For us, our walk had a bit of rough terrain (though we were lucky to come equipped with good hiking boots). For others, it's nearly impossible. As you start to strip away those privileges, the harder life as an aspec, and the harder coming out as aspec, can become. When you start adding different cultures, religions, races, ethnicities, ages, genders, and disabilities, that journey becomes more and more complicated.

In my Jewish family, there is a lot of pressure to have kids and get married because of histories of trauma related to the Nazi genocide, etc., and it feels hard to imagine disappointing my family if I want anything other than biological children. (Leah—she/her—queer, ace spectrum, homoromantic, demiromantic)

I am black. I am masculine presenting. That combo means I am not only expected by society around me to be sexual … but hyper-sexual. It's very difficult right now to be black and queer. There is homophobia within the black community to go around. It can be incredibly challenging to just … exist. (xtra.depresso—he/they—asexual, panromantic)

I come from a very liberal, progressive family that has always been very supportive of the LGBTQ community. Yet, the concept of split attraction and asexuality is still obscure enough that I feel that I don't know if they would understand. (Adriana Sage—she/her—asexual, heteroromantic)

I come from a very strict religious culture where chastity is strictly kept until marriage, and I believe that environment blurs my community's ideas of how the average person experiences sexual attraction. (Hattie—she/her—demisexual, heteroromantic)

My parents don't speak English very well, and I don't speak Chinese very well, so we just don't have the shared language to talk about these things. I do hope that they would, over time, just understand and accept that I have a long-term, committed preference to not date. (Susan—any—queer, asexual, aromantic)

I came out to my family as asexual around the same time I was, and still am, trying to get an autism spectrum diagnosis and realizing all the different little things I do that many people with autism also do ... So when I came out as ace my parents assumed that it was just me wanting to be autistic instead of accepting it as something I just am, autistic diagnosis or not. (Addie Byrne—she/her—bisexual, aspec)

I think the only person in my family who refuses to accept my asexuality was my twin sister. But she's always had issues with any differences between us. If she has interests in sex and dating then of course her twin should be like that too. That sort of toxic cultural idea surrounding twins that we should be natural forever besties and perfectly similar just because we shared a womb. It led us to be constantly compared to each other by society so every difference became glaringly obvious. (Rebecca W.—she/her—asexual, pan-greyromantic)

I am married and was married before I understood that I was asexual. Because of this, I haven't come out to hardly anyone besides my spouse. I feel like being married makes the conversation more complex with others, especially because it does push my spouse into people's minds as well. (Jess Shilling—they/them—asexual, arospec)

Though every coming out story is unique in its own way, there is one experience that feels near universal. "But honey," parents will say, "how will you have a happy family? What about kids?" The insinuation here is the same assumption put forth in Chapter 6, that asexual people cannot have sex. It may even follow the assumptions of Chapter 4, that aspec people cannot form romantic relationships or partnerships. We know that these assumptions are irrelevant. Aspecs have the same options for having a child as anyone else: sex, in vitro, surrogacy, adoption, fostering. And though it may be a shock to those who hold "traditional family values" so near and dear to their hearts, one does not need to be in a standard romantic–sexual relationship to have a child, or to have a family, for that matter. When we look at queer communities, when we peek through our aspec lenses, we see infinite possibilities for how to create a family, with or without children.

"Blood runs thicker than water." When we think about family, in the traditional sense that is, this is often the first quote that comes to mind. A proverb passed down from medieval times placed in front of us from birth that is meant to remind us of the importance of family, of *blood* family, above all else.

If you're queer, a purveyor of the found family trope, or just generally informed, you will know the true quote that this saying stems from: "the blood of the covenant is thicker than the water of the womb." The bonds we form by covenant, by agreement, by chosen bonds, are stronger than those formed through genetics.

Misquote aside, this concept is not altogether foreign in society or pop culture. Think for a moment about the characters from the biggest series of our time. The Golden Trio of *Harry Potter*, the Fellowship from *The Lord of the Rings*, the Cullens in *Twilight*, the "familia" so dramatically portrayed in the *Fast & Furious* franchise: these are all found families. They are groups with a common goal that act more like a family than a group of friends. Groups that are brought together not by blood, but by choice.

At the end of the day, however, these best-selling series and box office hits have not made the concept of found families any more socially acceptable. For many, it is simply a trope, a fantasy. When you tell your parents, or even your friends, that you want to buy a house with your friends and grow old together, they tell you to get real, to grow up. You aren't a child anymore; fantasies of hidden, underground tunnels from your house to your friends' should be put aside. But the aspec lens shows us that we do not have to toss that dream away. Just look at Reddit user Impressive-Jaguar and her friends, for example, as discussed in our chapter on friendship.

My ideal future has, for a number of years, been one in which I live with a close friend and at least one cat. I felt like that was a childish fantasy most people had "grown out of" until I found the aspec community and realized that it's not a silly thing to wish for. (Ever—they/them—asexual, aromantic spectrum)

For me, family is the people you choose to live your life with because they accept and love you for who you are. They listen when you talk about your experiences. For me, my found family is four adults (including me) in various romantic/platonic/? relationships who live together. We are all responsible for our own finances, but contribute to the household costs. We negotiate any long-term changes (like getting pets or long-term projects that take up space in the common areas). We have nights we set aside to spend time together, we take vacations together, we look out for each other. One day there might be children involved. We will not all be named parents, but we will all love and help raise said child(ren). Any future partners will be added to the family in whatever capacity they choose to be involved. For me, I do not think I will ever get married, so perhaps my partners won't live with me permanently. It works for us, and we are going to keep living together until it doesn't work (which I don't see happening for a long time, if ever). (Sara Talladira—she/he/they—asexual, pansexual)

I am part of a very close-knit climbing community and I consider many of them basically family. I spend Christmas with them, we camp out in each other's backyards, we let each other know when we're having "bad brain days." We take care of each other when a relative dies or someone breaks their leg. They bought me shoes once. It feels more like family than anything else so far and I'm deeply grateful for it. (Mic—she/they—asexual, lithromantic)

In 1974, the *New York Times* reported that one in every seven children in the US lived in a single-parent family. The growth of single-parent families was rapid at the time, outpacing the growth of nuclear families by seven times. Unsurprisingly, this raised some concerns, from worries about an increase in illiteracy to taboos surrounding divorce.[11] Luckily, others were in support, which is perhaps related to the continued rise of the single-parent family. As of 2021, a quarter of US children lived with only one parent.[12]

For aspecs who wish to become parents but aren't interested in or have trouble finding someone(s) to raise a child with, single-parenthood could provide an incredibly attractive option.

> I am currently in the process of creating a family of my own. I am trying to conceive using donor sperm to become a single mother by choice. It is one of the most exciting and terrifying things I have ever done and I cannot wait to continue this journey! I have a great support system of family and friends cheering me on and ready to help me in any way they can. It's a dream come true—proving the "love, marriage, baby carriage" way of thinking your life should go is obsolete! (Jessica Shea—she/her—asexual, aromantic)

But with dual-parent and nuclear families still reigning supreme, single parents can face a lot of barriers when it comes to building and supporting their families. Though there are many ways to have a child without a sexual partner involved, they are often incredibly expensive and/or time-consuming. Sperm donations, egg donations, and insemination procedures cost thousands of dollars for just one try at getting pregnant, and finding a surrogate can be just as hard as finding a partner. Adoption and fostering, on the other hand, can be a months- or years-long process—not to mention the fact that, at least in the United States, adoption is a largely for-profit, nearly 20 billion dollar industry.[13]

And life only gets more difficult after the baby actually arrives. Especially outside of Europe, parental leave is often woefully short. Childcare, if you can find it, is incredibly expensive and typically based around the idea that the child comes from a two-parent household. Society is just now catching onto the idea that stay-at-home mothers are no longer the default and that most families need two working parents just to maintain financial stability.

While single-parenthood still isn't 100 percent accepted (think pieces are still being written about the "single motherhood catastrophe"), we have come a long way since the 50s, 60s, and 70s—especially considering that structural supports are still sorely lacking for single parents, particularly for those who are financially underserved and/or a part of a disadvantaged minority group. Perhaps this is just a result of exposure therapy—after all, single-parenthood is far more common than it once was, with divorce rates constantly on the rise and financial independence becoming a more and more viable option for women in the past hundred years. But if our social order can evolve on this matter of family, why can't it also embrace other nontraditional types of families? What's stopping us?

For David Jay, single-parenthood was never an attractive option. In our interview with him for the 168th episode of the podcast, Jay said the following:

The struggle was never the biology of it, cause I was like, "there's so many ways to have a child in one's life, legally or otherwise." That part I'm not worried about. The part that was really challenging for me was the commitment part. I was like, if I can avoid it, I don't want to parent alone, not because that's not a great experience for many many people, but because it's a lot. If I can have support, if I can have people doing it with me, I think I can be a much better parent. I think I'm going to be a lot more happier and a lot more balanced.[14]

Jay has nothing against single-parent families, of course, but he knew that this option wouldn't mesh well with his lifestyle. So instead, he created a family that would work for him. In 2010, Jay met Avary Kent at a professional conference and they hit it off immediately. As they worked in the same industry, Jay and Kent became "intentional coworkers," sitting in coffee shops together to gain inspiration and bounce ideas off each other. Jay also became close with Kent's then-boyfriend, Zeke Hausfather.

After about a year of friendship, Jay sat down with the pair to have his classic intentionality conversation. This led to an even closer bond and found the trio taking trips and working together even more closely. Soon, Jay started dropping subtle hints that he was interested in having a child with the couple. He had known for years that he wanted to co-parent with a couple and thought Kent and Hausfather could be the people to make it work. The couple got married after some time, and soon after they sat Jay down to tell him they were thinking of starting a family and that they wanted him involved in a big way.

After a series of discussions, they decided that Jay would be an equal co-parent to the future child. As with all things David Jay, the planning process for parenthood was incredibly intentional. The trio discussed their family origins, worked out a schedule for parental duties and check-ins, and put together an entire "agreement document." When the child, Tavi, was born, Jay was ultimately able to become a legal co-parent to her as California had recently legalized third-parent adoption. Today, the trio lives together and co-parents their daughter Tavi, now in elementary school, in their home in San Francisco.

In September of 2020, asexual journalist Angela Chen wrote a piece on Jay and his family, as well as other advocates for alternative families, for *The Atlantic*. To the aspec community, this was a triumph. Not only was it a positive representation of aspecs in the media (and written by a fellow aspec, no less), but it was a positive representation of aspec *parents*. While so many doubt that aspecs can have children to begin with, this piece was proof that it is very much possible.

That isn't to say it will always be as "easy" as Jay's experience was. For starters, one has to find co-parents. For Jay, this took years. Forming bonds, be they platonic, romantic, sexual, or otherwise, can be hard enough for aspec people even without the burden of parenthood. There also comes the question of legality. While Jay was able to adopt Tavi as a third parent, this isn't an option in many places. Jay also explained to us in our interview that his privilege did help him throughout the process:

> And I have a lot of privilege. I have class privilege, I have other privileges. There are two types of family law, there's like rich people family law, which is managing divorces or privileged people family law, and there's other people family law, that's much more the state interjecting people. And just that mechanism wasn't pointed at me, but could very well be pointed at a lot of ace people and a lot of other legit families.

Jay also shared that because he isn't sexually or romantically involved with his co-parents, he breezes past many of the negative implications that poly families often face.

Whether they include children or not, polyamorous families are not yet fully accepted outside of the queer community—and even sometimes within it. However, they can provide amazing opportunities for many aspecs. For families that look more like Jay's, polyamory can allow for additional flexibility when it comes to parenting and childcare. Legal difficulties, as well as public perception of polyamorous families, are the largest drawback of this option. Unfortunately, not even Jay's story and Chen's article were without criticism from the media. Some value traditional families too much to imagine a world where a child has more than two parents. Which, when you break it down, doesn't exactly make sense. Children of divorce often have three or four parents when you take remarriages and stepparents into account.

But one does not need children to make a family, and plenty of polyamorous people make a family with their own partners, metamores,[b] and constellations.[c] While the outside world may view metamores as natural enemies fueled by jealousy, many polyamorous people have found their closest friends and found family members in their metamores. This doesn't happen for everyone, of course, as every relationship and constellation is different, but when it does happen it's beautiful.

---

b A metamore is your partner's partner who is not also a partner with you. It could be your husband's girlfriend, your girlfriend's girlfriend, your partner's boyfriend, etc.

c A constellation (sometimes interchangeable with the term polycule) refers to the collection of people who are in relationships with one or more members of a polyamorous group. For example, a constellation could be made up of you, your partner, your partner's girlfriend, your partner's girlfriend's boyfriend, your boyfriend, etc.

I would like to create my own family with one or more part-nerpeople and metamores. I'd like to live with a few of them in a house where everyone has their own room to be able to have their own space and I'd love it to be friends with them all. (Hat.schepsut—per/pers—asexual, arospec)

Our polycule contains four people—me, my husband Neil, my partner Scott, and my husband's partner Dan—and three distinct relationships. There are natural hierarchies due to prac-ticalities, but no relationship is relegated to "secondary" status. Each relationship is respected and nurtured by everyone else. And we all work at supporting the little family we've created. We call it "the constellation." Not only does it describe the way our individual points connect and form a whole, but Scott's an astrophysicist, so it seemed appropriate.

What I find beautiful about our constellation is that we get to love who we love exactly in the way we love them. Sometimes that's romantic. Sometimes that's platonic. Sometimes that's physical. Sometimes that's not. But it's all love. It's all family. And we're not constrained to heteronormative notions of what a relationship should look like. We build what works for us. (Cody Daigle-Orians—he/they—asexual, homoromantic)

For all this talk of alternative families, it is important to note once again that there is nothing wrong with aspiring to a "tradi-tional" nuclear family, complete with two parents, two and a half kids, and a white picket fence. Just as we asked you to analyze your partnerships, we ask you to analyze what you truly want in a family. If at the end of the day you want an escalator-esque relationship or "traditional" family, we will be the first to cheer you on in this endeavor. Because just by interrogating your ideas of family, you have already broken the mold. And hopefully, that will allow you to continue bringing intentionality, and the aspec lens, into your family as it forms.

> While my family is my husband and our two children, I am thrilled to have found aspec language and learned of the split model of attraction, because it gives my kids an expansive perspective around family. Rather than just saying banal things like "love who you want" and "family is what you make it," I can use ace words to get crystal clear about what I wish for them … that they choose who they love, how they love them, and that love doesn't just mean sex and partnership with kids at the end (insert all the aspec words there!). (Kate Gregory—she/her—demisexual)

And remember, just because your family may look traditional from the outside, this does not mean you have to adhere to the norm.

> My dream for my future family consists of a romantic partner and one or two kids. This is a pretty standard nuclear family, but the way that I approach finding a partner and imagine my ideal romantic partnership is inherently queer. I want all of the domestic family things, but within that, I picture my romantic partnership as a close friendship, plus all of the logistics of partnership. The line between platonic and romantic love for me is almost a conscious decision, to have someone that is my best friend, that I also want and choose to build a life with. (Autumn Brooke—she/her—asexual, demiromantic)

In writing this chapter, we have in no way covered every style of family, traditional or alternative. From multigenerational families to foster families to stepparents to our familial bonds with pets, we have not even begun to scrape the surface of what it means to form a family. There are also pages and pages that could be written (and have been by those more qualified than us) about the legal issues that come along with alternative families. In the eyes of the law in many places, only marriage and a birth certificate can prove family. For aspecs especially, this can make life incredibly difficult. For aspecs who are BIPOC (Black, Indigenous, and People of Color), low-income, disabled, immigrants, etc., the process only gets harder.

> The conventional meaning of family is flawed since there are legal scenarios that non-blood related persons have, that impact what is happening. My best friend is my emergency contact for health issues, however because we are not married, they do not have privileges that I would not give to my blood related family. (Alex Zafir Camacho Ocasio—any—trans, asexual, aromantic)

When we think about family in the 21st century, in Western culture at least, our ideas are quite rigid. But it is important to remember that this is not always what family has been. The meaning of family has changed over time and varies across cultures. Though it feels as though the concept of the nuclear family is cemented into the cultural zeitgeist, it has not always been and is not now the only form of family. We are of course not asking you to single-handedly break free from the ideals of the nuclear family; all that we ask is that you open your eyes to the fact that it is not the only way. Once you see the infinite possibilities that exist, you may just start to realize that anyone and anything can be family.

> Family as a First Nations person is everyone. The first thing you do when you meet someone new is trace each other's family trees back generation after generation to find out where you are connected, where the branches meet, where your roots entangle. I think that's a beautiful way of looking at family, especially as someone who doesn't intend to have children of their own, nor a partner in the colonial sense. Treat everyone you meet as family, and you'll never be without. (Pip—they/them—Indigenous Australian, asexual, aromantic)

Scan this QR code or click on the link below to access a bonus podcast episode about the making of this chapter.

https://www.soundsfakepod.com/sounds-book-but-okay-family

CHAPTER 7

Gender

To call gender complicated is an understatement. There is a great deal to contend with: the difference between gender identity and biological sex, the possible gender options that are even on the table (infinite), the gender roles and expectations that are so deeply ingrained in our culture and cultural practices, and the intersectional identities that often work to undercut or augment these "established" rules (i.e., Black women being oversexualized, Asian men being desexualized, disabled folks being nonsexualized, etc.). But before we wade too deep into the dismantling of gender through the lens of our aspec glasses, we're first going to start a bit simpler. That is, if you consider the intersection between aspec identities and the great mythical beast that is gender to be "simple."

In doing so, we're going to kick things off where the discourse on gender always seems to start and end: with men.

For asexual men, their sexual identity and their gender identity are often placed at odds with one another—not because they're inherently incompatible, but because the social expectations around them are so wildly different. Men, according to stereotypes and one-dimensional media portrayals, are meant to be hypersexual. Men, as a collective, supposedly exist in a boys' club that revolves around sex, women, and all things aggressively hetero: they go to strip clubs and hire prostitutes for their bachelor parties. They cheat on their wives with their secretaries because their wife isn't pleasing them enough and their secretary is just so hot, so who can blame them? They openly discuss their plans to "get lucky" over the weekend and share the dirty, dirty details with their buddies or their male coworkers come Monday morning Of course, even if men do aspire to live up to these stereotypical standards, the hurdles to achieving them are not equitable. An off-the-shelf white, cishet, able-bodied man will not have the same experience attempting to enter these boys' club spaces as, for example, a gay Asian man or a Black disabled man.

For asexual-spectrum men who either don't wish to out themselves or are still in the questioning phase, traversing these conversations and situations can be especially tricky. How to take part in them without drawing attention to their differences? How to get out of an uncomfortable and perhaps even unsafe interaction without drawing suspicion? How to integrate and become "one of the boys" without feeling, for lack of a better term, *icky*?

> Most of my male friends/peers/colleagues expect me to get involved with any chat about women, sex, etc. and I've had to get good at pretending to be interested in those conversations. (DN—he/him—asexual, h*ck knows re: romantic orientation)

Then, if or when asexual-spectrum men do come out, whether by choice or by force, they may be scorned by their male peers.

> The majority of my male friends I've come out to either did not believe me or wrote me off as an "incel." (Andrew Albert—he/him—asexual, biromantic)

113

For anyone blissfully unaware, incel is a term short for *involuntarily celibate*. There's significant baggage surrounding the term and its resulting community, but most important to note is that the textbook incel is a cisgender man who feels sexual attraction to women and wants sex, but for whatever reason, feels he can't get it. This is, definitionally and practically, nothing near the same as asexuality.

While some people proudly label themselves an incel, in more progressive circles, incel is used as a distinctly negative term. This is not, of course, because a sexless existence is shameful—if you're here, you know that to be untrue. The negative connotation comes primarily from the fact that incels are broadly known to be a sexist and hostile bunch. Since they feel a certain sense of bitterness and anger due to their supposed inability to attract a woman, most incels project this frustration and blame back onto women.

So, when asexual men are written off as incels, the implication is clear: it's more okay for a man to be a member of a community with a reputation for perpetuating violence against women than it is for them to identify as asexual. Perhaps in the eyes of some, at least if a man is an incel, they maintain some semblance of their masculinity (based, of course, in their attraction to and desire for women) that is not maintained if they don't feel the strong sexual pull supposedly characteristic of all men.

Although accurate and recent demographic information about the aspec community is rather hard to come by, it remains anecdotally true that in contrast to other gender identities, comparatively few cisgender men openly identify as aspec. And if men by and large are expected to be highly motivated by sex and sexual attraction, and shamed when they're not, it makes sense that few cis men would be eager to try on an aspec label for size—especially if they don't already identify as queer, and are thus already outside the norm.

Aspecs who were socialized as men, whether or not they ultimately identify that way, often feel a greater reticence to adopt aspec (especially asexual-spec) labels because of a highly gendered and subsequently highly sex-focused upbringing. Once they do, however, the aspec lens can start working its magic.

> In cultures or subcultures that put an emphasis on hegemonic masculinity, ace men like me have already broken through many barriers by rejecting that being sexually active is a masculine signifier. This makes it easier for us to reject social norms about gender and gives us greater freedom. (Lonely Wolf—he/him—asexual, aromantic)

These ace men, particularly cis ace men, also sometimes find themselves subject to an unintended side effect thanks to their sexuality: they aren't seen as a threat to women and trans/non-binary folks in the way that other men are. Because the most prominent threat men pose to people of these groups is primarily physical and sexual in nature, asexual men will often get a pass. This is not to say that aspec folks are incapable of or immune to committing acts of sexual violence or harassment. But to many people, the hypothetical threat of violence is significantly decreased when the person in question is aspec, thus making them a more trustworthy figure.

Plus, anyone identifying as aspec will probably have at least some grasp on the aspec lens and may be less beholden to toxic masculinity, another reason for women and trans/nonbinary folks to be more inclined to trust them.

> Once people get to know me better and are more comfortable around me, they know I'm totally safe as far as sex and sex talk goes. This has been kind of fun, as I found I've been let into

more "no guys allowed" social circles throughout my life. Kind of like the Gay Best Friend trope. (Soup—he/him—asexual, heteroromantic)

Alright, so what about those women? Women are expected to be less preoccupied with sex than men, and when they are open about their interest and participation in sex, it's considered taboo and unladylike. (Once again, we are speaking in broad terms here—understanding that there are nuances in how women are seen depending on their race, religion, socioeconomic status, health status, age, and more). As a result, asexuals who were socialized as women tend to have a very different relationship with their asexuality than those who were socialized as men.

As someone who grew up constantly being told "no sex until marriage," I easily took that to heart and was very confused why some people found that so difficult to do—in retrospect, this mindset probably delayed my personal realization of my asexuality. I had no desire whatsoever to do anything sexy with anyone, and thought that just made me the "good girl" I was conditioned to believe in. (Shannon—she/her—asexual, aromantic)

For many young acespec girls like Shannon, the abstinence-only approach to sex education (which is still so prevalent in many corners of society today) isn't hard to abide by. If they don't or only rarely experience sexual attraction and choose not to have sex because of that, they're able to keep themselves "pure"— without feeling any of the guilt that other young women are made to feel when they do experience sexual attraction or fantasies. They're doing what they *should* be doing, right? They're just doing it "better" than everyone else. It turns out that's simply because they don't necessarily have overbearing sexual attraction to contend with in the first place.

Once women are married, however, they face wildly different expectations. When there's a ring on their finger, women are supposed to be eager to have regular sex with their spouse, or at the very least they're supposed to be okay with it. For many women, this expectation expands even prior to marriage; as our social order evolves and grows slowly more progressive, it has become more and more acceptable for unmarried women to be sexually active. In an increasing number of communities, it's expected. But even here, there are still strict rules. For it to be considered socially kosher, a woman should be in a committed relationship with a partner before she has sex with them. At the very least, she should wait until after the third date before having sex with someone, because a woman who sleeps around and has one-night stands is too "easy."

So while young acespec men are made to feel bad if they're not experiencing a ton of sexual attraction and pursuing sexual relationships, many young acespec women have the exact opposite experience. They might grow up thinking they're just being "good," but once they enter a marriage or otherwise committed relationship where regular sex is expected, they're suddenly in over their head. According to the lore that pervades our world, they're supposed to turn on a dime, now experiencing a certain level of sexual attraction and/or sexual desire, and if they can't do that, they turn from "good girl" to "bad wife" very quickly.

And for those who find themselves in relationships and situations where they still don't feel the sexual attraction that's expected of them, they often hear the refrain that haunts every aspec: "You just haven't found the right one yet."

For some aces who do experience sexual attraction but

only rarely, this might actually be true. But in a broad sense, it's an incredibly harmful narrative. And due to the underlying romantic, though incredibly misguided, nature of it—that there is "the one" for every woman, whom she should ultimately give her entire self to—it is a narrative that is less often, though certainly not never, leveled at men. (We will, of course, return to the gendered notion of romance later in this chapter.)

When viewed as a collective, women are childbearers, valued merely for their output to society in the form of children. It is only on an individual level that they are sexualized, and this is almost always in the context of appealing to men and serving *their* sexual needs.

When individual women *are* sexualized (whether by choice or by force), there are strict rules about how they display their womanhood. For many, the cultural expectation that the way a woman presents themselves must be solely for the purpose of attracting men is a pervasive one. Any reader who was socialized as a woman will know that the moment they put on a smidge more makeup than usual or show any amount of cleavage, someone, somewhere, will ask them, "Ooh, who are you dressing up for?" When they're young and in their supposed prime for attracting a mate, girls are told not to cut their hair too short because it's too masculine, told to wear skirts and dresses at fancy events because it's ladylike. They must make themselves look as much as possible like the perfect child-rearing woman with wide hips and an ample bosom, so that they can have a man choose them like a prize cow at the county fair.

When we try to break down the myriad things that are wrong with this image, there are a *lot* of factors at play here—from hetero- and amatonormativity to good old-fashioned sexism and patriarchy. But there's also this idea baked into it all that there's a certain way to *be* a woman, which is informed in great part by how a person presents themselves physically. And if you've made it this far into the book, it will not surprise you to read that we find that concept to be absolute bullshit.

> I think being aspec and a woman frees me from a lot of the pressure I felt to uphold feminine beauty standards that cater towards "looking good for men." (PJ—she/her—asexual, aromantic)

The aspec lens reminds us that gendered beauty standards hold no basis in fact. It reminds us that no person, whether aspec or allo, needs to present their gender in a certain way *for* anyone but themselves.

And although this concept may often be thought of in the context of women "dressing for men," as we presented it here, you do not, of course, have to be a cisgender woman for this to apply. Any label comes with its own expectations about how a person of that gender ought to present themselves to fit the "ideal" of said gender identity, and the aspec lens teaches us to break away from the expectations of all of them. The evergreen tenet of *don't should* remains true regardless of the labels one uses: just as a cis woman need not meet a certain modicum of femininity, a trans person need not be "passing," nor must a nonbinary person present as androgynous.

A great number of aspecs of all genders, then, find themselves suffocated by the traditional notion of gender roles and presentation, and they may turn to feminism to find an example of how to break free of those established restrictions. For plenty of folks, that's enough. But on the other hand, a number of female-identifying aspecs actually find their gender identity at odds with the gender and sexual politics of modern feminism. This is based primarily on the complex, well-meaning, but often harmful intersection of asexuality and the idea of sex-positive feminism.

It is worth noting that some pockets of the aspec community do use the term sex-positive to describe what we would classify as sex-favorable—that is, a person (of any sexual orientation) who is favorable to and eager to participate in sexual acts. For the purposes of clarity as well as honoring our own personal terminology preferences in this book, we will use the term sex-positivity only in the context of sex-positive feminism, as we view it as a distinct and discrete concept from sex-favorability.

On the surface level, sex-positive feminism seems to align with values reinforced by the aspec lens: sex-positive doctrines preach freedom of sexual expression, action, and general liberation for women. But in practice, many sex-positive feminist teachings either imply or, on rare occasions, explicitly state that being a good feminist is actually about having lots of sex. It's about having as much subversive, kinky, queer sex as possible, because that's what most starkly goes against the status quo.

Alternate terms for sex-positive feminism include *pro-sex feminism*, *sex-radical feminism*, and *sexually liberal feminism*, each of which highlights that for many people, this mindset is not just about sexual freedom, but more specifically a pro-sex creed.[15] In fact, sex-positive feminism first emerged in opposition to more conservative feminists who were openly anti-pornography—in a sense, its origins lie in the promotion of sexual activity.

Whether this pro-sex interpretation of sex-positive feminism is correct or what its founders intended is not the point. What matters is how it comes across to potential practitioners, including those who are aspec.

There's a level of discomfort because I identify as a woman and a feminist, so I'm supposed to be sexually liberated and that's just obviously not for me. It makes me feel out of touch with some of the discourse surrounding women's sexuality. (Marie—she/her—asexual, aromantic)

While it's great to be sex-positive, in the midst of this hyper sexual culture sometimes I feel like a prude and like I'm a bad "liberated woman." (Sarah Brown—she/her—asexual, homoromantic)

In a way, being uninterested in having sex, or being aspec, feels like a betrayal of the women who fought so hard for sexual liberation not that long ago. It's playing into the societal expectation that women should be prudish vessels for men's sex. Obviously that's entirely false and bullshit to boot, but it can be hard to navigate my taught desire to be an ethical slut and enjoy sexual freedom in order to be "a Good Feminist" while also being inherently uninterested in having sex myself. (Morgan—she/they—asexual, demiromantic)

Sex-positive feminism is great, but what the aspec lens teaches us is that truly sex-positive feminism means that women not only have the right to have as much and whatever kind of sex they want, but also that the opposite can be true: that if a person doesn't feel compelled to have sex at all, no matter the reason, they don't have to. Choice is a spectrum that goes both ways.

Now, finally: let's *not* talk about sex, and instead bring the focus to romance. While the cultural zeitgeist expects "good" women to be pure and unmarred by sexual desire, the expectation for women around the topic of romance is the exact opposite. Starting as early as childhood, romance is something that little girls are supposed to eat up.

> Being aromantic as a cis woman is more difficult. Women, after all, are typically only seen as valuable in society if they are in a romantic relationship. You don't want to be an unmarried, single woman growing old or you'll be called "crazy cat lady" or some kind of witch or spinster. My internalized arophobia and general allonormativity made it much harder to initially accept my aromanticism. After all, I grew up as a little girl learning the narrative that I was going to meet a man and one day marry him on the best day of my life. I believed that for a very long time, so much that I accepted my asexuality long before my aromanticism because I just could not imagine not having that romance I was told was supposed to be the best part of my life. (Shannon—she/her—asexual, aromantic)

With this, heteronormativity once again worms its way into our discussion of gender. When heterosexuality exists as the "default," gender and sexuality grow to be practically intertwined, and we're left with incredibly pre-prescribed outlines for how they ought to interact with each other. Woman means romance-obsessed, man means sex-obsessed. Open and shut.

As such, when it comes to romantic pursuits, the allo- and amatonormative weight of the world is placed disproportionately on the shoulders of women. While men are free to hook up and pursue casual sex at will, pushing the sex-based portion of the allonormative agenda, it is women who bear the social pressure to carry the torch of romantic allo- and amatonormativity to pass along to the next generation.

Romance, especially committed romance, is expected to be a default lifetime goal for girls and women. The thought of a woman not wanting a romantic relationship, with any gender, seems to rub a lot of people the wrong way. Even "woke" people. (Lisa—she/her—asexual, greyromantic)

These stereotypes, based as they are in heteronormative gender roles, are so ingrained in our thinking and our understanding of gender that they remain even when the person themselves is not hetero or otherwise in a hetero-presenting relationship. As Lisa expresses, even those who might be considered "down with the gays" will often expect gay women to be more into romance and gay men to be more into sex. And if you're *not* into whichever of the two best matches your gender identity? Well, for many people that simply doesn't compute.

Often, aromantic-spectrum women will find themselves being compelled to reject "traditional" womanhood not because they have anything against it in particular, but because they so closely associate femininity with dating and romance. In these cases, it's not necessarily about a questioning of gender at all (although that can certainly be another layer of it), but about wanting to reject the stereotypes that surround gender.

I didn't want to date, so I didn't really want to do anything I associated with friends who were really into boys: beauty, fashion, baking, home decorating, etc. I've realized now that I wasn't trying to reject being a girl, I was trying to reject society's notion of what it meant for me to be a girl because, in my mind, that would involve dating. (LA—she/her—aspec)

So much of feminine identity has been about attraction, romance, and sex, so aro ace women essentially redefine womanhood in a queer way, even if we identify with our gender assigned at birth anyway. (Jenna DeWitt—she/her—aegosexual[a] aromantic)

Up until this point, we've focused primarily on the two binary signifiers of "male" and "female," since those are the ones society accepts into the fold, building its systems and frameworks accordingly. But as we've expressed time and time again, the point of adopting the aspec lens is to tear down those same systems and frameworks. When we ignore the boundaries of male and female entirely and realize that the rules and expectations that surround them serve no real purpose, it also becomes much easier to comprehend and embrace identities that fall outside of the cisgender norm.

> Coming to accept my asexual identity eventually facilitated my gender questioning ... Once my idea that sex was a requirement for the human experience was shattered, my idea that my gender had to be binary and align with my sex assigned at birth was also shaken. (Jasper—they/them—asexual, queer, greyromantic)

Jasper's experience—of beginning to question their gender only after and because they grew to understand and accept their asexuality—is actually a rather common one among aspecs. While some people certainly feel a disconnect with their gender

---

a   Aegosexuality is a sexuality on the asexual spectrum. Aegosexual people experience a disconnect between themselves and the object of their arousal. They may become aroused by sexual content (i.e., porn), but have no desire to participate in sex themselves.

and may identify as trans and/or nonbinary before they ever realize they're aspec, many others are able to use asexuality and/ or aromanticism as a jumping-off point. Once a person first puts on those purple-colored glasses and sees the potential a new mindset unleashes, it's understandable that they may not want to take them off. It's understandable that one may choose to embrace the unknown and the uncategorizable in contexts beyond relationships with one another and apply what the aspec lens teaches us to their relationship with themselves.

In fact, this particular phenomenon is one of the rare instances in the aspec community where statistics and data on the matter actually do exist, and the numbers are staggering.

The results of the Trevor Project's 2020 National Survey on LGBTQ Youth Mental Health indicate that 25 percent of the LGBTQ youth in their sample identify as transgender or non-binary, with another 9 percent questioning their gender identity. When looking solely at the respondents who identify as asexual, however, those numbers jump up to 41 percent and 13 percent respectively.[16] That means that when it comes to gender identity, more than half of asexual youth identify as trans, nonbinary, or otherwise questioning—putting cisgender asexuals in the minority. Though the study was limited to the United States, anecdotal evidence from within the aspec community indicates that this is likely an international phenomenon. Moreover, while the study was limited to asexuals, there is reason to believe this is just as likely to apply to any aspec-identifying person.

When discussing aspec folks who don't align with the well-worn cisgender binary, there is often special attention paid to those who identify specifically as nonbinary. Perhaps this is because nonbinary folks are often expected to present androgynously or without gender, and people draw a connection between this concept and the aspec notion of being without attraction. The lived experience of nonbinary folks, however, often does not match up with this mindset. Certainly some people—specifically, those who identify as agender—may feel they are genderless. But while agender is generally considered to fall under the broader nonbinary umbrella, that's a one-way street. Being nonbinary does not make you automatically without gender.

As such, insisting that nonbinary folks present androgynously or in some other manner deemed genderless is actually just reinforcing the constrictive gender expectations we already have. Our aspec glasses show us how we can tear down the walls between male and female, not how to build another wall that merely adds nonbinary as a third acceptable gender (or lack thereof). The goal is to transcend the bounds of gender, not create more of those same boundaries. As a result, those aspec folks who do identify as nonbinary often have to do a lot of dispelling of assumptions.

> Most people have this idea of an ace enby[b] as someone trying to strip themselves of gender signifiers, when I want to be more than I am. I want to be colorfully, ridiculously me, and being ace is part of that. (Darcy R.—they/them—asexual, panromantic)

Most nonbinary folks, aspec or not, are not trying to rid themselves of any sort of gender identity. They are simply building a new type of gender identity, just as bold and human as any other. It's not a dissociation from humanity, but a brave attempt to craft a new, more inclusive kind of humanity to add to the bunch. No greater or lesser, just different.

Still, some aspecs, once they've seen gender through the lens of their aspec glasses, don't feel a strong connection to it at all.

---

b   Enby is often used as shorthand for a nonbinary person.

It's not just about being unconnected to the gender which they were assigned at birth, but a general apathy towards the institution of gender as a whole.

> I think that a lot of gender roles are constructed around sexual attraction, and not having sexual attraction is kind of why I don't have a strong association with gender. (Em A.—they/them—queer, asexual)

Along these same lines, many aspecs may not explicitly identify as trans and/or nonbinary, but find themselves to be fairly pronoun-indifferent nonetheless.

> I personally care little about my gender identity … I still present as a woman and use she/her pronouns but that's only because it's what I'm used to and what people see me as. I don't feel particularly attached to the woman gender or the pronouns. It would not bother me at all if people did not use she/her pronouns. (Lex—she/her—asexual)

> I identify as a cis man, but that's mostly just because it's convenient. I'd rather let whatever/whoever I happen to be define my masculinity, than let my masculinity define what/who I become. I always put he/him as my pronouns (again, mostly out of convenience), but I'm ultimately fairly pronoun indifferent I think. (Jonathan Freeman—he/him—asexual, aromantic)

Some aspecs also find themselves wanting to distance themselves from the parts of their gender or presentation that are sexualizing—or parts of their bodies that are not sexual by nature but often sexualized within the broader culture.

As breasts are heavily sexualized in every form of media, I was never comfortable with my own. Even crossing my arms didn't feel right because I preferred to simply forget that they existed. (Finch—she/her—asexual, aromantic)

For those aspecs who also identify as trans and/or nonbinary, the intersection of those two identities can be especially complex and have any number of varying effects.

I am nonbinary/genderqueer and I feel like my gender is very tied with my ace identity. I think it took me such a long time to figure out my gender because I'm ace. I thought that I was uncomfortable looking like a girl because of how sexualized AFAB bodies are by general society. (Mattea—they/them—asexual, aromantic)

A lot of my ace identity is inherently a part of my trans identity. Being sex-indifferent or sex-repulsed is fueled by my lack of sexual attraction and my disconnection from my body. One example is that my aversion to wearing a bikini stems from not wanting people to be sexually attracted to me, but also that it accentuates the parts of my body that I am most uncomfortable with and what I see as counter to how I view myself. (Kara T.—they/them—asexual, arospec, queer)

I am nonbinary and I feel that my gender dysphoria may be part of why I am sex-averse. I feel that there is a pro in that being asexual means that I am not distressed by any sex-aversion I experience due to my gender dysphoria. (Em Z.—they/them—asexual, biromantic)

I definitely think that some of my asexual identity is influenced by gender dysphoria and general discomfort or dissatisfaction with my body. However, I don't see myself becoming "less asexual" even if I decide to pursue surgery at some point. (Becca— they/them—asexual, biromantic)

Me being transmasc and not having genital dysphoria might be a result of being asexual and sex-repulsed. Like, no one is going to see that, so it doesn't matter. (Nic—he/they—asexual, lesbian-oriented)

Ultimately, when we cross aspec identities with gender and look at both through the lens of our aspec glasses, the result we get is just the words "DON'T SHOULD" in blinking red letters. We hope that at this point, this is not a shock to you. Applying the aspec lens to your gender, even (or perhaps especially) if you *are* cis, means accepting that the rules don't matter, and the only one who gets to decide what your gender is and how to present it is you.

The way you identify can also change from moment to moment. Our many identities are interconnected, and those who have found themselves changing their labels over the course of their life know that better than anyone.

As we briefly mentioned in Chapter 4, one of our survey respondents, Phoebe, actually stopped identifying as aspec at some point between submitting their response and when we reached out to get consent to use two of their quotes. She explained that her no longer identifying as aspec likely had a lot to do with her identity as a trans woman—and how her experience of her sexuality changed after beginning their transition.

I had identified as ace, and I think I truly was, prior to my transition. I could come up with a laundry list of possible causes, but what I liked about the asexual label was that it denied that sort of questioning. It was all-encompassing and non-pathologizing: I could simply say "I'm asexual," be understood and (hopefully) respected. Finding a community of other ace people who navigated amatonormativity, too, was massively beneficial to embracing myself authentically, even if I would one day leave [that community]. Now that I have (and in some ways still am) transitioning, I've felt strong sexual attraction. But one thing I've [taken] away from all this is that there's nothing good or bad about that. It's simply another experience I can explore or not explore, rather than some cosmic narrative I'm supposed to follow. And I also have the language to describe it on its terms, too, and I may need those labels again one day anyhow! It makes my relationships, sexual or otherwise, way better—and I'm forever grateful for that. (Phoebe Langley—she/they—bisexual)

Phoebe's experience serves as a stark reminder to all that identity is fluid, and just because they no longer identify as aspec doesn't mean that their experiences—or her responses to our survey, for that matter—are any less valuable. Embracing the aspec lens benefits everyone, even those who don't currently identify as aspec.

Although we've hit on several different topics in this chapter and approached gender from a number of different angles, we will leave you with the following quotes to remind you that once you have a grasp on all of those purple-colored perspectives, combining them and integrating them into your own life isn't as complicated as one might expect. The practical application, of course, is not always easy. We will not pretend that publicly rejecting the bounds of traditional gender expectations is a walk in the park. But despite the complex nature of gender and the way it interacts with aspec identities, with a bit of time, understanding it through the context of the aspec lens can actually come as second nature.

Realizing I'm aspec has helped me to feel more liberated in the way I dress and express myself. I've come to realize that a lot of things I did as a woman I did to please especially the male gaze, like shaving or having long hair. I feel like it's helping me to define for myself what it means to be a woman and not have that dictated by other people. (Annina—she/her—acespec, arospec)

Agender living just takes me off the planning board and that gives me a chaotic freedom that is very much akin to my view of aromanticism and relational anarchy. (Rai—they/them—gyne-phile, gynosexual,[c] lesbian, trixic,[d] aromantic, alterous)

It is strange because a lot of expectations in relation to gender come from traditional views and traditional relationships with people from the same and other genders. If you don't follow those traditional relationships, a lot of the expectations of a certain gender cannot be applied to you anymore (regardless of what people often expect or push on you). I have noticed that it can put you apart from people of the same gender as you, because you don't have the same experiences in relation to your gender and people of other genders. These experiences are often seen as typical for women or men and if you don't experience these, it can make you wonder what makes you your gender. This

---

c   A gynosexual is someone who's attracted to femininity. This is regardless of whether or not the person in question identifies as female, and solely about expressing feminine characteristics.

d   Trixic is a term which describes someone who is nonbinary and attracted to women.

is not necessarily a case of being trans (I am a cis woman), but it makes you wonder why everything is so divided and defined by binary gender and gender roles. (C. Vdb—she/her—asexual, aromantic)

All gender really is, in the end, is the perceived difference between people. Traditionally, there is the male category and the female category, and they are defined only in opposition to each other: without man there is no woman, without woman there is no man. So, if you look at gender and take away the experiences that are meant to differentiate between them—in this context, traditional relationship roles—what are we left with? Nothing but a bunch of loosely grouped characteristics that aren't actually grounded in any known reality.[e] It's no wonder a disproportionate number of aspecs identify as trans and/or nonbinary—once we become familiar with the aspec lens, of course we start applying it elsewhere. It would be incredibly difficult to throw out the arbitrary societal rules in one aspect of our lives but happily uphold them in another.

Much like the rest of our structures and institutions, when examined through the aspec lens, the strict boundaries of gender simply crumble.

---

e Obviously there are distinct differences in the physiological characteristics of what we call male vs. female genitalia—but those are in reference to biological sex, not gender.

Scan this QR code or click on the link below to access a bonus podcast episode about the making of this chapter.

https://www.soundsfakepod.com/sounds-book-but-okay-gender

CHAPTER 8

Miscellanea

Because the possible applications of the aspec lens are practically limitless, this book could potentially reach encyclopedic levels of length. But we do not have the time to write that, nor do we assume many (if any) of our readers would have the will to read such an infinite document. So instead of boring you with everything that ever was, we'll leave you with just a few of the many additional topics that stand out to us when considered alongside the aspec lens.

Housing

We touched upon the idea of an aspec approach to housing a bit in Chapter 3, where we discussed the living arrangements of Reddit user Impressive-Jaguar, but in doing so we only barely dipped a toe into all that could be. Obviously, buying adjacent properties with one's friends is by no means a realistic option for many—scratch that, most—people. Although single-family home ownership was a flagship achievement for middle-class Baby Boomers, the cost of housing in the 21st century has sky-rocketed to a point that for Millennials and burgeoning Gen Z'ers, home ownership is a luxury. For many, it's nothing but a pipe dream. This is especially true for individuals who expect to be single as they age.

We would be remiss not to also highlight the fact that while home ownership may have been standard for some Baby Boomers, this was by and large limited to white folks. In fact, many—if not most—BIPOC communities have been long left behind by and legally excluded from traditional single-family housing institutions. Their lived solutions provide a good example of how it might be possible to break the broader culture free of the white picket fence mold.

While Western cultures view living in one's parents' basement as a distinctly bad thing, in many Asian and Latin cultures, multiple generations living under one roof is the norm. As a result, members of those communities who have immigrated elsewhere in the world tend to be far more open to multigenerational living, making the associated taboos less pervasive.[17] In an interview with *BuzzFeed News* in 2020, one woman, Mina, noted that because of her Middle Eastern heritage, moving back home to live with her parents at the age of 40 was less shameful than it might otherwise have been.[18] Living with her parents again was certainly a complicated change for Mina, but as an immunocompromised person living in a global pandemic, it meant having the benefit of a wider safety net when it came to her long-term health.

For others, living with family isn't an option, so they look to do something similar vis-à-vis a shared home with their friends. Couples sharing a house or apartment with other couples or even single friends is becoming increasingly common, and it's hardly difficult to imagine that trend expanding as time goes by. If people can't afford to move into single-family homes, the normalization of communal living will be unavoidable. What the aspec lens suggests, however, is that we normalize such a lifestyle not just for those who can't afford to do anything else, but for anyone who sees value in living this way, regardless of their economic background. The aspec lens suggests that we view it not merely as a last resort, but simply as another option.

Still, while community is undoubtedly important, we need not share a bedroom with our entire extended community if that's not the right path for us. Sarah, for example, is an introvert to whom truly communal group living sounds like an absolute nightmare. She would love to live alone with a small commune of dogs, but as an underpaid, rent-burdened resident of Los Angeles, at this time that's just wildly unrealistic. Hopefully, she'll someday reach a point where a roommate-less life is an option (no offense to her wonderful roommate and her beloved cat), but that day certainly won't be any time soon.[a]

What if you don't want to live with a ton of people, but can't afford to live alone—not just as a young person first entering the workforce, but also in the long term? Well, that's a valid question. To be truthful, we wish we had a better answer for this, but we don't. We can only hope that as we don our aspec glasses and tear down the hetero, monogamous, couple-centric structures of our world, we will also find space for more affordable living options for those who already do or otherwise wish to operate outside the so-called "norm," aspec and allo alike.

---

a   Unless this book miraculously sells 10 million copies.

Kink

At first glance, kink is all but synonymous with sex. In fact, you may be wondering to yourself why you're reading about it here, rather than in Chapter 5. You may also be wondering why kink is in a book about asexuality at all. We can't blame you for these questions. As always, it is society that's to blame. If our broader culture was inclined to provide any concrete information to the lay person about what kink *actually* is, we wouldn't need to include this section of the book at all. But alas.

Before we share the perspectives of our survey respondents and talk about why aspecs might participate in kink, let's first define it. Our good friend Wikipedia defines kink as "the use of non-conventional sexual practices, concepts, or fantasies."[19] This definition isn't necessarily wrong, but it doesn't paint the full picture either. Contrary to popular belief, kink does not always have to involve sex. While kink often involves sexual acts in combination with things like power play, role play, bondage, etc., it doesn't have to. Those acts can be performed without sex and still be kink. Just as sex is an activity that can be performed without attraction, so too can kink be performed without any sexual aspects. There's nothing stopping you from doing a little power play with a play partner without any sexual implications. In the end, it's just an activity.

Unfortunately, finding a definition of kink that encompasses these many varied practices is not easy. It took a fair bit of digging for us to find a definition that we liked and felt properly encompassed the many nuances of kink, but eventually we landed here: "'Kink' is a broad term that refers to a wide variety of consensual, non-traditional sexual, sensual, and intimate behaviors such as sadomasochism, domination and submission, erotic roleplaying, fetishism, and erotic forms of discipline."[20] This definition, which encompasses practices that are sensual or intimate, rather than just sexual, is much more inclusive of the varied ways to practice kink.

All this being said, what's in it for aspecs? Why do aspecs participate in kink in the first place? Well, the answer that first jumps to mind would be sexual gratification (for those who participate in the sexual aspects of kink). Just as aspecs can enjoy sex, aspecs can enjoy kinky sex. But for those who take sex out of the equation, what's left?

For starters, sexual pleasure is not the only kind of physical pleasure for us humans to enjoy. The physical aspects of kink (hitting, bondage, rope play, etc.) can still feel good without being sexual in nature.

> I enjoy [kink]. Another activity that feels good. I enjoy the pleasure I feel from [it] but again, it's more about connection and trust and intimacy than sex. So I feel like it shouldn't inherently be sexual since most times it doesn't lead me and my partner to have sex, just a fun game we play. (Alexis M.—she/they—asexual, panromantic)

Pleasure can also move beyond the physical, with kink providing mental respite for others.

> For me kink isn't a sexual practice. It's about intimacy and communication. I am autistic and words can be really hard and

impossible sometimes but kink is a way for me to communicate without words. (Frances—xe/xem—asexual, aromantic)

Bondage is also a very non-sexual practice as well. As someone who deals with depression and anxiety, doing a bondage scene can be very grounding and brings me into the moment. It goes back to what has been consented to. (Sierra—she/her—asexual, aromantic)

Intimacy and trust, mentioned above, are key tenets of the kink community. Not every kinky person is into or comfortable with the same activities, which makes communication and consent paramount. For many, the process of talking about sex and what you do and don't like can be awkward. Sharing sexual preferences isn't something they teach in "sex ed," so many of us are left clueless. But in the kink community, these conversations are not just encouraged, they're part of the culture. This emphasis on communication relieves a lot of the ambiguity around sex and provides partners with clear guidelines as to what they want. For aspecs who may have more boundaries than an allosexual person, this can be especially helpful.

I was particularly drawn to the very thorough practice of negotiation in kink, where play partners openly discuss boundaries that can be very specific: "You can touch me here, but not there," "We can do this thing, but my clothes will stay on the whole time," etc. ... It's way easier to discuss my aro/ace-related limits around intimacy with another kinky person because play partner relationships already require a much higher level of communication than vanilla relationships. (PJ—she/her—asexual, aromantic)

Kink for me has its rules. There's the arranged time, place, and process. Having that script makes sex-related activities make sense to me. I don't necessarily understand the desire to do sex acts with others because I don't have that attraction, but within the rules of kink, I feel secure in my role in those acts. (Matt Thomas—she/he/they—asexual, pansexual)

Getting into kink has actually improved my current relationship—building restraint and denial into our sex life as well as explicit consent has meant that everyone's needs get met and communication has improved. (Ruby—she/they—asexual, demiromantic)

I also really really really like the idea of "checklists" in kink, where rational discussions of boundaries and activities are discussed before engaging in any sexual play. As an ace person, I have absolutely no idea how people just "go with the flow" during sex or nonverbally communicate or enforce sexual boundaries. There seems to just be generalized assumptions that allos make about the people they're sleeping with and what those people want and are okay with that I don't understand at all. It kind of freaks me out. (Elizabeth—she/her—asexual, heteroromantic)

Kinky or not, BDSM or kink checklists, the kind that Elizabeth mentioned, can be incredibly helpful when it comes to physical and/or sexual boundaries. A cousin to the BDSM test that you and your friends may have taken online while bored at the dining hall, kink checklists can include physical activities from hand holding to knife play and anything in between. Even if you don't participate in sexual activity, checklists can be an incredibly helpful tool when entering into a conversation about physical and/or sexual boundaries.

If you're interested, do a little Googling around "kink check-lists" or "BDSM checklists." It may take some time to find or create one that fits your specific needs, but it can be a perfect format for discussing boundaries of any kind in any type of relationship. Left to flounder by the woefully inadequate "sex ed" curriculum taught in schools, we'd advise taking any help you can get when it comes to making consent and boundary conversations a little less awkward.

While kink and kink culture provide a lot of benefits to the aspecs who participate, it doesn't all come easily. As kink is largely seen as a sexual practice and asexuality is largely seen as a sexless identity, the two communities don't always mesh well.

> Sometimes it feels as if I'm doubly marginalized, because within kink there may not be an understanding of asexuality and within the asexual community of course there are a wide variety of people with different places on the spectrum who may not understand kink. (Sarah Brown—she/her—asexual, homoromantic)

> I don't think being aspec hinders my ability to experience kinks, though it does give me anxiety and paranoia when it comes to explaining it to others, again because of the common misconceptions that kinks are inherently sexual and therefore counteract being aspec. (Eliott Scott Simpson—he/they—asexual, panromantic)

As long as the socially accepted definition remains the same, as long as we keep sex centered in our conversations about kink, kinky aspecs will continue to feel this dissonance. And just as we have said for the entirety of this book, it is not just aspecs who are disadvantaged by society's strict norms and centering of sex and romance. The taboos surrounding kink impact kinksters and vanilla folks alike, putting unnecessary rules around the right and wrong ways to gain physical pleasure, whether that involves sex or not.

But when we put on our aspec glasses, when we view kink in the way that kinky aspecs do, we not only find the infinite ways to benefit from and enjoy kink, we also begin to understand kink's place in the world. Not as something strange or shocking, but as another way to build intimacy and learn from those around us.

Media

When we reconsider the lens through which we view our lives, that also means allowing that lens to reshape our conception of everything adjacent to our lives—and that includes things like the media we consume. As it pertains to mass media, a number of things become apparent once one becomes familiar with aspec identities. The first and most glaring is that there is very little representation of aspec identities outside of our self-built communities.

This is in reference to both real-life representation (aspecs being open about their identities in the workplace, aspec voices and narratives being highlighted in daily life, etc.) as well as representation of aspec identities in fiction. While IRL representation can be improved with the spreading of information about the aspectrum and the normalization of aspec identities, fiction can get a little more complex.

The lack of inclusion of aspec characters and stories in mainstream fiction is not just because people don't know about the identities or that they're taboo, although both certainly play a significant role. Another reason for their lack of inclusion is because many people (falsely) believe that these characters are "less interesting." After all, much of the drama in TV, film, novels, comics, manga—any medium, really—is rooted in some way in romantic–sexual relationships. We've got the classic love triangles, the will-they-won't-they, the star-crossed lovers. Even if a story is not specifically about romance or sex, there is almost always a romantic–sexual element to it as a B story. And of course, this element typically fits cleanly into the heteronormative mold. To illustrate our case, take major English-language films.

Seeking examples of romantic–sexual storylines in sci-fi? Any installation in the *Star Wars* or *Star Trek* franchises will do. Horror films? How about *A Quiet Place* (2018) or *Friday the 13th* (1980)? Heist films? Any of the *Ocean's* trilogy. Westerns? *Django Unchained* (2012). And as for superhero movies? Do not ever, *ever*, bring up *Avengers: Age of Ultron* (2015) around Sarah unless you're willing to get into a long discussion about abrupt, out-of-character, and frankly offensive romantic subplots that get shoehorned in because someone, somewhere, insisted that there be one.

We'll stop now because we could do this for days, but our point is merely that romance and sex are pivotal aspects in every genre. Even for movies directed at kids and family-friendly films more generally—notable examples being the ever-dominant Disney princess movies—it has only been in the past few years that they have begun to move away from including romantic plots as a rule. And while aspec stories and characters are becoming *slightly* more common in television (we now need two hands to count all the shows instead of just one, which is a huge feat), at the time of publication we aren't familiar with a single mainstream, non-self-funded film that features aspec identities.

We'd like to once again emphasize that we are by no means anti-romance or anti-romantic plot. Both authors, after all, are verified stans of *Pride and Prejudice* (2005). But the fact remains that it's nearly impossible to find stories without deeply embedded romantic–sexual plotlines, and it's in large part because of that same precedent that folks continue to be reticent to tell stories about aspec characters. Plenty of aspec characters could, of course, still have romantic and/or sexual relationships, but this is often seen as too complicated or too difficult to convey.

Those wearing their aspec glasses, however, will know that just because a love story is not based in traditional romantic–sexual dynamics doesn't mean it's not interesting or worth telling. There are plenty of incredible stories to tell about platonic and familial relationships that are just as intimate and dramatic as any other, whether they involve aspec folks or not.

Of course, complex aspec representation is also incredibly crucial, and there is so much to unpack here that we could write a whole other book on the topic. In fact, many wonderful aspec writers and researchers have delved into the subject far more than we could even dream of doing here, which is why we'll keep our exploration of this particular point rather simple: mass aspec representation is important not just so that burgeoning aspecs can feel safer and more comfortable in their identities, but also so that allos learn what aspec umbrella identities are.

As we've said time and time again throughout this book, the aspec lens is not just for those who identify as aspec; it's for everyone. Tearing down the structures that can prove harmful to aspecs also serves allos—both on an individual level and as a broader society. The more often the general public sees and hears positive, accurate representations of aspec identities, the greater the understanding they have, and the more likely they are to slip on a nice pair of those purple-colored glasses and possibly even join us in the work to change our systems. In the end, this benefits us all.

This image of allos of all stripes becoming invested in aspec content and causes brings us to an important point to be made about media more broadly—because the aspec lens teaches us not just to reconfigure the way we think about the stories we tell, but also the way we consume those that already exist.

The thing about media is that in most cases (especially here in the 21st century) we can return to the same texts time and time again. When we do reread a book, or rewatch a movie, or relisten to an album, however, any time that has passed since the last read or watch or listen leaves a mark on us. We are not the same people when we return to beloved childhood stories as an adult. We are not the same people when we return to beloved adulthood stories as an adultier adult.

Sometimes this has a positive effect: maybe we see the intricacies in a film we didn't quite grasp in our youth, or we catch some of the subtle adult humor and get a good laugh. Sometimes it has a negative effect: with the benefit of all we know now, we realize that some piece of media is, in fact, very problematic. Sometimes it's as simple as a plot point hitting a little different now that you've experienced a certain life event, or as complex as looking at a film's pseudo-science and saying, "I know now that all of this is wrong and here is a 12-page essay as to why."

Learning about the aspec lens and putting on those glasses often leaves a huge impact on the way we consume media. While wearing your aspec glasses, for example, you may notice that the vast majority of songs are about romantic and/or sexual love.

You may more intensely feel the heteronormativity ingrained in 90s rom-coms—or even the rom-com that's in theaters right now. You may discover that so many of the seemingly innocent tropes in our zeitgeist rely upon harmful stereotypes.

It's not always this cut and dried, but learning to apply the aspec lens to the media we consume is all about learning to question it and think critically about it. It's realizing that those who created this media are just as incredibly pressured by society's status quo as the rest of us, and the art that results reflects that.

Along these same lines, another important lesson to be learned from embracing the aspec lens is how to be discerning. Revisiting the media we used to love in our youth, for example, and finding aspects of it problematic, does not negate any other positives we may have gleaned from it. It also does not necessitate casting it aside entirely (although in some cases it certainly can).

JK Rowling's views on gender do not take away from the hope and comfort so many trans people have gotten out of the *Harry Potter* books, films, and resulting communities, nor does it mean that the themes of her books which trans folks have felt paralleled their own experiences are no longer valid. Realizing that a classic comedy contains homophobic jokes doesn't mean that no joke ever told in the movie is funny, it just means realizing some of them definitely aren't.

We are by no means trying to tell anyone that they must stick with something upon revisiting it and finding holes in it. If leaving it behind seems like the right course of action for you, do it. But utilizing your aspec glasses to their fullest extent sometimes means putting things in a larger context. The bad is still bad even if the good outweighs it, but if we tossed aside every piece of media that didn't pass some aspec version of the Bechdel test, we'd be left with almost nothing.

The aspec lens merely gives us a set of tools for deciding what can stay and what must go in our own personal Rolodex of media, as well as ideas about what types of media we hope to support and uplift going forward.

Beyond

English speakers have long used the phrase *rose-colored glasses* to describe viewing the world through an overly, and often falsely, optimistic lens. There are times when viewing the world through our purple-colored glasses feels like the exact opposite.

When we look through the aspec lens, we see that the world is a horribly prejudiced place. We see that it's at best inconvenient and at worst actively hostile to anyone who exists outside the status quo—whether they're doing so by choice or by force. For some people, observing their surroundings through the aspec lens may, above all else, actually inspire a feeling of hopelessness. Wearing your purple-colored glasses can sour your experience of the world, because it does the opposite of what rose-colored glasses do: it forces you to strip away the comfortable, childlike innocence of it all.

But wearing purple-colored glasses is not just about seeing the world as it is, with all its faults and flaws, but also how it could be.

Because the aspec lens also teaches us that the bounds of love, family, community, and self are not so limited as the narratives we hear as young people might lead us to believe.

The aspec lens teaches us that—to quote Drew Carey on *Whose Line Is It Anyway?*—"everything is made up and the points don't matter." It teaches us that humanity is vast and complex, and although our social order and the resulting legal frameworks may do everything in their power to force us to do otherwise, we are welcome to build our lives and our own personal worlds however we goddamn please.

In the very first sentence of this book, we posited that the aspec story is a love story. That they all are, in the end. And what we hope you can see by now is that the reason for this is because love is not limited to romance or sex or that nebulous thing called attraction.

Ultimately, to love is to care.

And if there is anything that the aspec doctrines teach us to do well, it is care. So many aspec folks have at one time or another felt like an outcast because of the way we experience the world, so we care that those around us are comfortable in their skin and in their relationships. We care so much about understanding ourselves and one another that we, as a community, have created an entire arsenal of terms and titles and words to describe our identities. We care to build a world where all people, aspecs and allos alike, feel safe to explore and *be*, not limited by the confines of a rigid and arbitrary status quo.

The way aspecs love may be a bit different from what is expected of human beings, but that does not make it any lesser. Every aspec the stars have ever touched is so profoundly real and complete and human, and to be human is to love. To be human is to love is to care, and our aspec lens teaches us nothing but.

As we established at the very beginning of this book and emphasized throughout, we won't pretend that adopting the aspec lens, that somehow managing to fuse those purple-colored glasses onto your face, is easy. But aspecs and allos alike have a lot to learn from adopting this perspective, and if you've made it all the way to the end of this book (congrats! thanks!), you've already taken the first several steps. So keep going, dear reader. You can do this. We wish you the best of luck, wherever your journey takes you.

Oh, and for the love of all things good: *don't should.*

Scan this QR code or click on the link below to access a bonus podcast episode about the making of this chapter.

https://www.soundsfakepod.com/sounds-book-but-okay-miscellanea

References

* Please note that we are using this with permission from the Estate of Gloria Watkins (bell hooks).

1. Brake, E. (n.d.) Amatonormativity. Last accessed January 29, 2022 at https://elizabethbrake.com/amatonormativity

2. Cohen, R. (October 20, 2020) What if friendship, not marriage, was at the center of life? *The Atlantic*. Last accessed May 31, 2022 at www.theatlantic.com/family/archive/2020/10/people-who-prioritize-friendship-over-romance/616779

3. Palazzo, N. (June 21, 2021) Platonic marriage carries legal risks. *The Herald Journal*. Last accessed May 31, 2022 at www.hjnews.com/opinion/columns/platonic-marriage-carries-legal-risks/article_20b5ed70-5bb8-56f0-a3f8-197d815792a6.html

4. Nordgren, A. (July 6, 2012) The short instructional manifesto for relationship anarchy. *Andie's Log*. Last accessed May 31, 2022 at https://log.andie.se/post/26652940513/the-short-instructional-manifesto-for-relationship

5. ideacity (August 13, 2015) David Jay: Asexuality [Video]. *YouTube*. Last accessed May 31, 2022 at www.youtube.com/watch?v=VLIo9O8bMkU&t=1s

6. Impressive-Jaguar (2020) AITA for putting my single best friends before my married ones all the time? [Online forum post]. *Reddit*. Last accessed May 31, 2022 at www.reddit.com/r/AmItheAsshole/comments/eyqwy8/aita_for_putting_my_single_best_friends_before_my

7. Hopper, B. (February 26, 2016) Relying on friendship in a world made for couples. *The Cut*. Last accessed May 31, 2022 at www.thecut.com/2016/02/single-ladies-friendship-romantic-fraught.html

8. Gahran, A. (2017) *Stepping off the Relationship Escalator: Uncommon Love and Life.* Off the Escalator Enterprises. pp.3–4.

9. Gahran, A. (2017) *Stepping off the Relationship Escalator: Uncommon Love and Life.* Off the Escalator Enterprises. p.19.

10. Gahran, A. (2017) *Stepping off the Relationship Escalator: Uncommon Love and Life.* Off the Escalator Enterprises. p.216.

11. Dullea, G. (December 3, 1974) The increasing single-parent families... *The New York Times*, 46. Last accessed May 31, 2022 at www.nytimes.com/1974/12/03/archives/the-increasing-single-parent-families-lack-of-day-care-unawareness.html

12. U.S. Census Bureau (2021) Historical Living Arrangements of Children [Data file]. Last accessed May 31, 2022 at www.census.gov/data/tables/time-series/demo/families/children.html

13. IBIS World (May 2021) Adoption & Child Welfare Services Industry in the US—Market Research Report.

14. Costello, S. and Kaszyca, K. (Hosts) (January 31, 2021) Episode 168: Asexual parenting feat. David Jay [Audio podcast transcript]. *Sounds Fake But Okay*. Last accessed May 31, 2022 at https://soundsfakepod.buzzsprout.com/218346/7573522-ep-168-asexual-parenting-feat-david-jay

15. Wikipedia (n.d.) Sex-positive feminism. Last accessed May 31, 2022 at https://en.wikipedia.org/w/index.php?title=Sex-positive_feminism&oldid=1069775964

16. The Trevor Project (October 26, 2020) Asexual and ace spectrum youth. Last accessed May 31, 2022 at www.thetrevorproject.org/research-briefs/asexual-and-ace-spectrum-youth

17. Binette, J., Houghton, A., and Firestone, S. (2021) *Drivers & Barriers to Living in a Multigenerational Household Pre-COVID–Mid-COVID.* Washington, DC: AARP Research. Last accessed May 31, 2022 at www.aarp.org/research/topics/community/info-2020/multigenerational-multicultural-living.html

18. Bogart, L. (September 28, 2020) Millennials are trying to shake the stigma of moving back in with their parents. *BuzzFeed News.* Last accessed February 22, 2022 at www.buzzfeednews.com/article/laurabogart/millennials-moving-back-in-with-their-parents-adulting

19. Wikipedia (n.d.) Kink (sexuality). Last accessed May 31, 2022 at https://en.wikipedia.org/w/index.php?title=Kink_(sexuality)&oldid=1062881549

20. Aaron, M. (n.d.) Growing up kinky: Research shows how kink identity is formed. *Psychology Today.* Last accessed February 4, 2022 at www.psychologytoday.com/us/blog/standard-deviations/201805/growing-kinky-research-shows-how-kink-identity-is-formed

Acknowledgments

First, we'd like to say thank you to our editor, Andrew James, for actively seeking out aspec voices and giving us a platform to share them. It means more than we can say.

Thank you to the Estate of Gloria Watkins (bell hooks) for the use of our epigraph.

Thank you to our listeners for giving us the platform that made this book possible. We often wonder why you came to us and why you've stayed, but we're incredibly grateful that you have. Your support, your listens, your emails, and the community you've built have been our greatest motivation.

To our fellow aspec activists, writers, and creators for pushing us to be better, for being a constant inspiration, for educating us and lifting us up. Our work is difficult, but we're honored to share this community with you.

To all of our survey respondents—thank you for your vulnerability and honesty. We could not have written this book without you.

To the little Airstream we stayed in on our writing retreat in Texas and also the chickens that lived there, though they were not much help.

To Cherry Coke and Mountain Dew and Cinnamon Toast Crunch and Mike and Ikes—the fuel of any great writer.

To the University of Michigan housing algorithm in the fall of 2015—for picking our names out of the bunch and putting the two of us together in Alice Lloyd Hall, Room 4005. We would be nothing without you, you sweet, serendipitous little 1s and 0s.

Kayla

My first thank you must go to my mom, dad, and sister Rachel, who sparked my love of reading and writing early in life. Thank you for your willingness and eagerness to continue to learn and understand as my identity has changed. Thank you for turning into teachers yourselves, for championing my causes, for lifting me up rather than hiding me away. Few are as lucky as me. I am grateful for you every day.

Thank you to Dean, my loving partner, for countless dinners cooked, drives made, tears dried, and storms weathered. No workaholic is complete without a partner to gently nudge them away from the computer and outside of the house for once. Without you, this would not have been possible. You are the perfect ally.

To Billie and Gnocchi, the cutest freeloaders to ever exist. I wish you'd pay the rent, but thank you for the cuddles either way. (If you bite this book like you do all my others, I will be sending you back to the streets.)

To Monique, for being the voice of reason amid a sea of

imposter syndrome and anxiety. For encouraging me to use my doubt as inspiration, rather than as a hindrance.

To Laura, my newest baby aspec. You were in the back of my mind the entire writing process. I hope you learned something new about yourself within these pages.

And finally, to Sarah for, well ... everything. For being my perfect twin and perfect opposite. For, blessedly, not sharing my insecurities and doing your best to talk me out of them. For not caring what others think. For not being scared away when I puked on our first day of college. For teaching me how precious friendship truly is. For teaching me to not should. Without you, I would not know myself. Without you, these words would not have been written. Without you, where would I be?

Sarah

Thank you first to my parents for your unconditional love and support. Even when you didn't quite understand, you took it upon yourselves to learn, and I am incredibly grateful for that— if only every queer kid could have parents like you. And thank you in particular to my mother for being a better promoter of my podcast and book than I could ever be.

Thank you to Emily for paving the way for me as the second queer kid—you are the reason I was never afraid. Also, thank you for bringing Rosie into my life. (I am not even joking. I love that dog so much. Please tell her I miss her.)

To Miranda—thank you for being the friend who became family. Thank you for being the one who will never judge me.

To BTS, who I am absolutely shocked and disturbed to realize I didn't even mention once in this book. Thank you for making me want to be better. There were many, many days where the only reason I wrote was because you inspired me to create.

Thank you to whoever rejected me from the University of Michigan Honors College, because it was you who brought me to Kayla Kaszyca.

On that note ... Kayla. Kaaaayla Kayla Kayla. Words cannot express. Thank you for suggesting we start a podcast. For being the one constant when everything else goes to shit. For your patience when I didn't work on this book for months at a time. For understanding me. For being the one who perhaps knows better than anyone else in the world how annoying I am, and loving me not just in spite of it, but because of it. You are a writer, and this book is just as much yours as it is mine. If you ever doubt that, I will punch you in the face. (It'll hurt my wrist and it'll hurt your face and it'll be embarrassing for both of us, so seriously, please just don't.)

And finally, thank you to little Sarah. And big Sarah, and every Sarah in between. I'm so proud of you. I hope you're proud of me.

Last but certainly not least, we'd like to acknowledge you, dear reader. There is nothing about you that is broken or wrong. The world may be cruel, but you are a wonder. Even if your life does not follow the beaten path, you deserve happiness, security, and peace, and anyone who tries to tell you otherwise can answer to us.

Index